Pawn Takes Castle

PAWN TAKES CASTLE

by

Bunty Kinsman

ORIEL PRESS

© 1971 Bunty Kinsman
First published 1971

ISBN 0 85362 132 2
Library of Congress Catalogue Card No. 77-152522

Published by Oriel Press Ltd.
32 Ridley Place, Newcastle upon Tyne, England, NE1 8LH
Set in Bembo and printed by
The Kynoch Press, Birmingham

To Anthony with Love

Contents

1 We Buy a Castle

LONDON 1961.

The August sun shone on to the flagstones of our small garden. They in turn flung back a blistering heat. With one part of my mind I heard our four children squabbling together. Why was it that children were always at their worst in the heat, just when one wanted to relax? Perhaps the London summer seemed even more oppressive owing to the fact that my husband Anthony and I had just returned from our annual holiday. It had been spent in the West Country on our usual unavailing hunt for the perfect home. Some time previously we had decided that we had lost our appetite for London; anyway it was no place for children to grow up in. We felt that a quiet rural life away from smog, traffic queues and supermarkets was what we needed.

Querulous small voices were now demanding a walk to the Serpentine. Absently I assented. Already I was mentally arranging the pram, canopy and sun-bonnets. I was retrieving bootees, putting leads on our Saluki and whippet . . . in short, assembling all the paraphernalia for our daily pilgrimage. I sighed, and made to put away *The Times*. Then an idea occurred to me: "I'll just finish this anagram before we go."

And it was my passion for crosswords that ended the

hunt. The pencilled letters of my anagram were neatly surrounding a small advertisement:

FOR SALE

Historic Border Castle *on the shores of Lake Ullswater. The mediæval thirteenth century building is scheduled as an ancient monument. Traces of the moat are still visible. There is a King's Room, so called because it is believed that in 1131 William of Malmesbury stated that it was the place where Constantine King of Scots, Eugenius King of Strathclyde and Athelstan, and the King of England met to sign a treaty placing themselves under the protection of England.*

"It sounds just the thing for us," I said.

Anthony's voice was rather dubious: "The price is right, but we'd starve. We haven't enough capital to farm, and London is where the money is."

"We could live more cheaply in the country," I argued. "And it would be a wonderful place for children to grow up."

I had gained a point. We both agreed that our family was outgrowing our small house. We certainly did not want them to become London children, nanny-ridden little molly coddles, with pale faces and too-clean clothes.

"Think of it," I continued. "No more traffic jams, no more queues, no more net curtains to keep out the smog."

Anthony was becoming more enthusiastic:

"No more rush hours on the tube, no more walks in Hyde Park, no more business lunches in sleazy city restaurants. . . . It's certainly tantalizing. But the place would be impossible to run with a midden instead of a 'loo'."

"Well shall I just ring the house agents for an appointment?" I asked cajolingly.

When I had replaced the receiver I murmured to

myself the name of my new find . . . Dacre Castle. Yes
it definitely had a nice ring about it.

. . . And this was the home which two years later we
were to share with our Saluki, two whippets, peacocks,
falcons, a donkey, three horses, a raven and a large
floating population of pigeons, wild duck and homing
budgerigars.

Of course, instead of going to Kensington Gardens I
went straight to the house agents. The kindly paternal
man who greeted me was wary and discouraging. A
twenty-two year lease was to cost £1,500, with a
nominal rent of 5/- a week. I waxed ebullient in my
enthusiasm . . . yes indeed, here was a country house
we really could afford. I hardly noticed that the house
agent had more the mien of an undertaker than of a
man with a prospective sale on his hands. Lugubrious
phrases bounced like pellets into my mind and straight
out again:

"A gloomy ruin . . ."

"In a bad state of decay . . ."

"Extremely bleak . . ."

"A conversion must be carried out by the lessee," he
continued. "The two great halls must become reception
rooms, with three bedrooms and two bathrooms being
created out of the rooms in the turrets. You'll have to
make a kitchen too," continued my Job's comforter
ominously, "although as far as I can see there isn't any
place for one . . ."

But I was gazing at a photostat cutting from a magazine 40 years old. In the blurred picture I saw an ancient
keep, gaunt and grey. Its sole pretensions to design were
four diamond-shaped turrets and some crenellated
battlements; its sole decoration a few stunted, wind-
blown trees. In the background, just discernible, was

what Anthony termed "real country." Already my mind was made up.

We had two days of our holiday left. By midnight my husband and I, two dogs, four children and their goldfish were on the sleeper to Penrith.

We walked to the hotel in the cold of early morning, with the wind in our faces. At *The George*, all old oak and polished pewter, we discovered that the only bus service to Dacre was once a week, on market days. As this was not a market day we decided to take a bus to the nearest point, the village of Pooley Bridge, which was situated at the northern end of Ullswater. From there we planned to walk across country. Our goldfish was left in the care of an apple-cheeked maid. It looked very much at home in the centre of a large refectory table.

It was raining in a steady drizzle as we climbed out of the bus. Apart from two fishermen in oilskins hunched in a rowing boat, the lake was deserted. The placid water, bordered by green meadows and wooded hills which stretched away to the gaunt heights of Martindale, looked enchanting to concrete-clouded London eyes.

Turning up the collars of our coats we consulted our map and set off towards our *El Dorado*. The going was heavy and the children were beginning to drag at my arms. Anthony was carrying Sebastian who was then only three months old. Half an hour's plodding through dripping woods and across sodden fields brought us out on to a road and abreast of a signpost. Quickening our pace we soon reached the brow of the hill and saw that we had gained our objective. Staring at the view we realized how Stout Cortes must have felt, when from a peak in the Darien he first glimpsed the Pacific Ocean.

Below us snaked a broad stream spanned by an ancient hump-backed bridge, while on the opposing slope of the valley, among a green kaleidoscope of trees and hedges, lay the hamlet of Dacre. It appeared at first glance to be a mediaeval village. There was no shop. Only a few slate-roofed cottages, a tythe barn, and a thirteenth century church backed by sable yews to complete the illusion and sanctify the scene.

At that moment, as if by some deliberate theatrical effect, the clouds parted, and the sun shining through spot-lit the tall protective walls of the castle which loomed over the village. Four crenellated turrets set diamond-wise at the angles of a crenellated cube, it had the stark symmetry of a child's drawing. The walls, polished by centuries of time, glowed with a mellow purplish patina, much softer than the red sandstone of the ruined castle we had seen at Penrith. But there was no softness in the overall effect which was rather of massive and enduring strength.

From his pocket Anthony took a silver flask which had sustained four generations of his family, and we each had a swig of whisky before I broke the silence:

"It looks rather tempting," I suggested.

"It looks irresistible," Anthony replied firmly.

In the village a rutted path branched from the road to the castle.

It looked incredibly old and calm and quiet. "How many trials it must have withstood in its day," I thought, "and how strange that border raids, wind, snow and tempest should all have spared it and left it in peace." We passed an empty and overgrown moat which led to rough stone steps and the front door. This was a green shoddy affair of fairly recent construction, and quite unworthy of its setting. There appeared to be no lock or handle and a slight push sent it creaking grudgingly back on its hinges.

The scene which met our eyes might have come from one of Samuel Becket's less lighthearted plays. The main prop, so to speak, was a majestic lavatory pedestal which dominated the stage from an unscreened recess in one wall. There were also two broken chairs and a chipped earthenware sink, with a single dripping tap.

Gingerly we walked across wooden boards which had been gnawed into great holes by rats; in fact in many places it was possible to see 20 feet down to the dungeons below. The hall had massive smoke-stained beams which had once been hung with hams and cured mutton; between them dangled strips of plaster like the tattered pennants of a beaten army. The stones of the walls were bound together with moss and lichen, but in places someone had mistakenly tried to patch them with ugly khaki splodges of cement.

The noble fireplace, six feet in height, was filled with a sullen looking iron range, scarred with rust, which almost hid the ancient bread oven. A stone piscina, with scalloped font, was let into the wall beside the front door; we discovered later that this had once been part of a small chapel. One of the windows was mullioned. The others were plate glass, broken where birds had flown in.

The whole effect was undeniably depressing, and yet ... and yet ... The proportions of the room were truly magnificent.

"Evidently living with history has its drawbacks," Anthony remarked dryly. "There seems to be no telephone, bath, washbasin, or for that matter any hot taps."

A little deflated we climbed the gloomy newel stairs.

The effort of making this staircase must have been prodigious and the masons' marks on the enormous stones still proclaimed the identity of the mediaeval craftsmen. We were interested to see how it spiralled upwards towards the right, so that the defenders could carry their swords in their right hands. Small short-eared bats hung to the rafters and I nervously clutched at my hair, until we reached the sanctuary of the King's Room.

I must here admit my Irish ancestry; perhaps this is why the story of the bats grew somewhat in the telling. A few weeks later there was a paragraph in the *Express*:

"*Lloyds broker Mr. Anthony Kinsman whose wife Bunty is one of London's most assiduous partygivers, is planning to make Dacre Castle his home, at a peppercorn rent of £10 a year. This may sound a splendid bargain but Dacre is far removed from the Kinsmans' usual surrounds. For though it has four turrets, dungeons, moat and drawbridge, it has no bathrooms or sanitation. The ceilings are held up by tree trunks and there are bats the size of bulldogs flying about, says Mrs. Kinsman . . .*"

Jokes die hard in the heart of the country and it has taken us many years to live that one down.

The King's Room was a ruin indeed. The broken flagstones on the floor were interspersed with patches of cement. The castle was built on two floors so that this room was directly below the roof, which was supported by beams resting on stone corbels. In one corner a corbel had come away from the wall and the weight of the beam was supported by a large tree trunk set up like a tent pole. The room was vast, but years of decay seemed to have crept with the moss and stonecrop into the darkness of its crannies. There was a curious smell about the place, apparently caused by the bat droppings which lay about the floor like piles of small shot.

7

Some time later in a musty volume obtained from Penrith library we learned how the castle had come into being. Dacre Castle so the book stated, was possibly once a monastery built of wood and shingle, referred to by the Venerable Bede in 730.

The stone peel tower in its present form had been built by William de Dacre, who became the first Lord Dacre, early in the fourteenth century.

In Edward II's reign William de Dacre obtained a licence to have the house crenellated. Margaret de Dacre, who eloped when she was 17 to marry William's son Ranulph, had permission when widowed to construct a chapel inside the castle in 1354. In 1485 a curtain wall was built.

Down the ages this ancient peel tower had known splendour and decay. Writing in the seventeenth century, the Cumberland antiquary Edmund Sandford spoke of its solitary position and appearance: "*From Matterdale mountains comes Daker Bek: Almost at the foote thereof stands Daker Castle alone: and no more houses about it: and I protest looks very sorrowfull.*" In spite of the eccentric spelling and punctuation this passage gives a very clear impression of how Dacre looked when we first saw it.

By the second half of the seventeenth century the castle had passed to the Lennards, and Thomas Lennard Earl of Sussex had "*the very faire ancient fabrik*" repaired, and put his coat of arms over the new entrance. "*There are three stories in goode repair by the Earl of Sussex who, I believe, louves it well*", wrote a historian of the day. And it was the Earl of Sussex, we read, who had enlarged the mediaeval slits in the castle walls to square framed windows and fitted them with mullioned panes, thus "*making his residence more genteele.*"

8

There is also an amusing anecdote about this Earl. One of the tiny rooms in the East Turret boasts a genuine Norman latrine, and this room was once the Earl's guardrobe. Here he would sit for many hours, watching the farmland which was once his deer park, enjoying the sight of his deer being hunted round and round his palings.

Looking back, I am certain that it was the munificence of Lord Sussex concerning the diamond-paned windows which influenced our decision to buy the lease of Dacre Castle, for at the first sight of the breathtaking view we forgot our doubts.

The castle is set in an amphitheatre of wild fells, backed by even wilder mountains. From one window we saw the east fells with the snowcapped Pennines in the distance; from the other Red Crag and Whitestone Moor. Climbing higher on to the battlements we glimpsed a tongue of azure lake against the backdrop of towering larch which crowned Dunmallet. This view completed the sense of timelessness. Dunmallet we knew had once been a Roman Camp, whose guardians had bent the knee to Jove and Mars.

From this moment caution was hurled to the four winds. It was a blissful moment of hope, comfortingly blinded from the vicissitudes that the coming months would bring. But then my life with Anthony had always been governed by snap decisions. Often they were the wrong ones, but if we have a philosophy it is this—as you only have one life, you might as well get the most out of it. Such an outlook does not make one a millionaire but it does a great deal to vanquish that sophisticated ogre of the twentieth century — boredom.

Back in London, friends were incredulous at our

determination to leave the glittering life of the city for this bleak Cumberland ruin.

"You'll be back in six months," they said.

"You'll never stick it . . ."

"What on earth will you do with yourselves ? Won't you be bored?"

And plaintively, remembering our annual parties: "What shall we do on New Year's Eve?"

How to explain what to them appeared our misplaced enthusiasm? How to explain that we were tired of the rat race, the tinsel frivolity of our lives? How to find words to describe the weariness of our tight little world of cocktail parties, charity balls and first nights? We seemed to be spinning endlessly on one spot. We were leading the same life with the same friends as last year and the year before . . . the only difference was that we were all getting a little older.

We had managed to knock £500 off the premium, and Dacre Castle was nominally ours. But it was two years before we were able to move in. During those two years we had to sell our London house, for repairs to the castle were proving even more expensive than we had thought. This first severance with the old life hurt me more than I had expected.

40 Smith Terrace was only a converted slum house in Chelsea like so many others, *chi-chied* up with the usual flag-stoned terrace, fish pond, brightly painted front door and ornate knocker (ours was a particularly pretty one, bought from an antique shop near the Parthenon in Athens). But behind those pale stucco walls lay five happy years of our life.

I could not help feeling that some of the gaiety and happiness of our lives would survive within the rooms. Here we had entertained so many dear friends, held so many parties. Tropical parties, oriental parties, Russian parties with vodka—and just parties.

As we made our final exeunt, with children, trunks and baggage piled into a taxi and a pantechnicon full of furniture outside, I turned to look for the last time at my little drawing room. The sun shining through the front door harshly spot-lit the scene, showing the dusty yellow marks on the walls where the pictures had been. How well I remembered when those walls, hung with murals to emphasize the various themes of our *beat-ups*, had rung with snatches of gay conversation, tinkling glasses and laughter. Then some of the stars of my fleeting recollections were again in the empty room, sharply lit in the diamond brilliance of this sunny morning.

Frozen against an oriental background were some of the most beautiful and elegant women of our time. There were famous models: Anne Gunning, Shelagh Wilson, Jean Dawney and Marla Landi. Sharmini Tiruchelvam, Annigoni's "most beautiful girl in the world" looked on at the scene from her lovely doe-like eyes. She was wearing her own genuine sari, dripping with gold embroidery. There in another corner were Zinnia Pollock, Denise Kilmarnock, Sarah Aberdare and Bronwin Astor, dressed as pretty geisha girls, looking as if they had just stepped out of Madame Butterfly.

Then my shifting memories revolved the stage to another party in winter, a black tie affair this time. Flowers were hard to come by in London at that time of year and I had created some terrible floral decorations copied from pictures in a woman's magazine. All over the room were dotted one or two flowers twined round red candles amongst hideous bunches of white doyleys.

Suddenly I saw portrait painter Nicolas Egon waving to me frantically over the heads of the crowd: "Bunty darling, your doyleys are on fire "

At this party my only true floral arrangement was a bowl of orchids sent to me before the party by one of the guests, an Italian. How I love this thoughtful continental fashion of sending flowers before a party; it is such a help to the flurried hostess. The pretty Italian authoress Gaia Servadio came to this party and wrote it up for her paper in Rome. *"Bunty's walls,"* she eulogized, *"were lined from floor to ceiling in orchids!"* I loved this. It made me feel as if I had just stepped out of the pages of de Sarde.

Another turn of the revolving stage and there, flood-lit in the sun, was our tropical party that we gave with George Weidenfeld and Michael Alexander. Now it was summer with flowers everywhere, raffia skirts and brown bodies dancing to *Main Stream*. There was Jane Vane-Tempest Stewart, normally a blonde but on this night a dusky Spaniard, George and Diana Melly looking splendid as a sheik and a slave girl, and Feliks Topolski, a perfect beachcomber in his customary artist's sweater and grey flannels.

Then my mind guided the spotlight to other more formal evenings. The colours were softened to the warm glow of candlelight. Centre-back there was a group of men in dinner jackets. Charles Clore, Michael Lewis, who since those days has become owner of the *Queen* magazine, the Duke of Prima de Riviera, prior to his tragic death a few years ago, William de Gelsey and Duncan Sandys were all deep in serious conversation. By the fire Michael's elegant wife Gloria in something chic by Balenciaga, Caroline Leeds, Mary Quant, Pat Harmsworth and Franchesca Ruspoli chatted to me, and sipped their brandy, their dresses spread about them like the petals of flowers.

Preserved in this room were so many fragments of other people's lives, forgotten perhaps by them, but to be remembered by me, I hoped, for many years to come.

2 Bills Galore!

A CHARMING and elegant young bachelor bought our house, complete with curtains and carpets, and hand-painted Chinese wallpaper. The only change that he intended to make was to the rather dilapidated basement nursery; it was to be converted to a dining room with pine-panelled walls.

To find a furnished flat was easier said than done. Smart London landlords do not consider a couple with four children and two dogs the best of tenants. In the end we were reduced to the subterfuge of sending Anthony and our daughter Amanda on ahead in the pretence that this was all the family consisted of. Once the lease was signed the reserves would move in, and the landlord would be presented with a *fait accompli*. This was not an unmitigated success, and in all we moved five times during these two years. The standard of our homes kept getting progressively lower. Smart flats in Kensington and Chelsea were exchanged for sleazy maisonettes in Fulham and Bayswater.

During this time I think the pace of our vertiginous existence tended to increase. From our flats we orga-nized our last two New Year's Eve parties. For the first we took over the beautiful Theatre Royal Stratford (East, not Avon) home of Theatre Workshop, for an Arabian party. A Siberian party would have been a better choice.

The *Evening Standard* wrote the next day:

"*Bunt's party starts the new year in fine Arabian style . . .
not even the worst of winter deterred 300 people from
dressing up in Arabian costume for a pulsing affair.*"
Paul Tanfield's column in the *Daily Mail* headlined
with:

"*Bunty takes over a theatre to say Hello 1962!*

*In a skidding taxi, slithering from one side of the road to
the other, I zig-zagged across London last night to drink a
glass of champagne at some of the gayest New Year's Eve
parties going. True, hundreds of guests didn't have my brave
driver, and couldn't pick their way through the freezing
slush, but those who did turn up made the most of the
occasion. Furthest flung of London's parties was the fancy
dress one thrown by Mrs. Bunty Kinsman who appeared as
Cleopatra. Her guests danced on the stage before a back-
cloth of Puss in Boots. 'Wish I'd worn boots,' grumbled one
Mayfair oriental through her sodden yashmak, as she hung
her Dior stockings on a radiator.*"

Indeed it was the whitest of white New Year's Eves.
All the afternoon the radio had been telling us that it
was dangerous to use our cars, but by that time it was
too late to cancel the party. The B.B.C. had already
set up their cameras and some of our friends from the
country would already be on their way. Most of the
yashmaks were frozen solid on our guests as they
pushed their cars out of snow drifts on the journey
homewards. I am afraid that some of the cars would
not move, or if they did it was only to skid into other
cars, and the road from the East End to Chelsea was
literally paved with refrigerated Arabs.

The next year we gave our final party in Crosby Hall,
a great mediaeval barn of a place that we had hired for
the night.

According to one newspaper:

"Mrs. Bunty Kinsman Bossa Nova'd into 1963 in naught but a diamond-spangled bikini, a pair of mink eyelashes (15s. from Harrods) and a yard or two of white organza." Next morning with a bad hangover I surveyed the William Hickey headlines:

"Brazen, blizzarding, 1963 sweeps in.

Well, whoopee! If you have enough energy left to raise a cheer, 1962 snow-flaked out and 1963 came brazenly, blizzarding in. Ex-Grenadier Officer Anthony Kinsman and his wife gave the best party of both years at Chelsea's Crosby Hall. The guests turned up in mediaeval dress to be greeted by Mrs. Kinsman dressed as a unicorn and Mr. Kinsman puzzlingly attired in the fur cover from a baby's pram. I'm a middle-aged wolf," he explained . . ."

"New Year . . ." said another paper, *"came in with a blare of trumpets."* But to me, my mediaeval party, myself included, had resembled a rather worn-out pack of tarot cards which had been too often re-shuffled and were becoming a little worn.

On New Year's morning too, the bills for converting the castle started to come in to confirm that the party was truly over.

Mr. Unwin, the architect we had chosen, was a talented, good-looking, down-to-earth Rhodesian. He had evidently studied the castle with the eyes of practical knowledge, unlike Anthony and myself, who had only seen it with the eyes of wishful thinking. He always wrote to us in green ink, and how I grew to dread those green type-written envelopes.

His first letter was full of *no*'s. There were *no* doors, *no* floors worth keeping, *no* larder, *no* linen cupboard, *no* window panes, *no* heating system, *no* kitchen, *no* bathrooms, *no* lavatory unless we wanted to use the one

Dacre Castle—*home* to us!
Photo. Eric Davidson

Discussing life with Edward
Photo. Daily Express

The King's Room—showing the North Window
Photo. Eric Davidson

that was sitting so majestically in the middle of the hall . . . How many of these items did we require?

With an uneasy sense of foreboding we had to admit that we required them all. There was only one bright spot in all this. Mr. Unwin was adept at obtaining grants, and the local authorities agreed to spend £100 on doing up one room, as long as it was used as a larder. I was rather pleased by this unusual stipulation. I had never had a larder, and had delicious visions of a return to Victorian living, with well-stocked shelves full of meat safes, whole salmon and stilton cheeses.

The next grant that we managed to obtain was from the Ministry of Works. Dacre Castle was apparently scheduled as an ancient monument and the Ministry agreed to contribute a third of the expense, but on structural repairs only. A condition was that we should open the castle to the public for fifteen years. Blithely we agreed, for who would be likely to visit us in such a remote place? Little did we visualize the stream of tourists who would arrive in the summer, usually when I was cooking a meal, bathing the baby or trying to curl my hair. But the Ministry was reasonable about this, as indeed it has been about everything. It agreed to allow us to open the castle by appointment only.

It only had one criticism of our improvements, and thinking it over I believe it was right, although it was a dreadful blow at the time. When the moss and algae had been cleaned from the stone walls in the King's Room, the walls had to be repointed with cement. Now the builders, whom Mr. Unwin had found for us, made a perfect job of it, but according to the Ministry it was too perfect. The cement was flush with the stones, destroying their look of antiquity. A veritable army of men had then to be employed at our expense to gouge a great deal of the cement out again. It must have been heartbreaking work.

Mr. Unwin told us to our delight that the great slates on the roof were better left alone, although all the lead gutters had to be renewed. The rat-gnawed floorboards also had to be torn up. This our workmen did, replacing them with planks of South American pine, which now after five years, thanks to the administrations of Mrs. Wells our local farmer's wife, glow with the colour of deep golden honey.

About this time the builders found a priests' hole in the King's Room. It was a small room only 7 feet by 4 feet, concealed behind the fireplace and the external wall. This was an exciting find and the room coincided with a minute stoned-up window on the west façade of the building. Unfortunately the expense of restoring the priests' hole was too great and it had to be blocked up once more. However Anthony and I often tell each other that perhaps one day . . . I think though it is more likely that the priests' hole will remain a thrilling discovery for future generations.

The cement splodges in the great hall had to be removed and the whole room, which was 45 feet by 30 feet, had to be plastered. Unhampered by doors and windows the wind and rain had taken their toll and the drying-out process and replastering was likely to be a heavy and expensive job.

The letters in green type were now coming thick and fast. One of them had an ominous postscript. It was suspected that the alcove that had been dug out for the lavatory had weakened the whole structure of the west wall. In another week the blow fell. The west wall was definitely unsafe. But apparently the Ministry were used to this kind of thing. The wall must be grouted with hundreds of tons of cement, a specialized job—the cost £1,000. Still reeling from this blow we received yet another. The stones by the south window in the King's Room were crumbling. These had to be renewed. The masons did this job so brilliantly that the new stones are now indistinguishable from the old.

With all these technical difficulties Mr. Unwin's practical knowledge was proving invaluable. The only access from the hall to the top of the castle was the newel staircase which wound upwards from the dungeons to the battlements. Vaguely we had decided that this would be adequate. Mr. Unwin insisted that it would not; he thought it impracticable and dangerous. We dreaded the thought of any structural change in the castle, and three sections of the oak beams had to be removed. But when Anthony visited the castle a few months later he said that the new staircase was a great success, blending in beautifully with the rest of the decor, in the same honey gold wood as the flooring. To my mind now, it even makes the two rooms more interesting.

When Lowther Castle was gutted some years ago, the elaborate iron door hinges were stored in builders' warehouses in Lowther. We arranged with Mr. Russell, the managing director, to buy them, and they have given our new oak doors an impressive air of antique authenticity.

The expenses entailed on all these items were making us extremely uneasy. I now visualized the portcullis of the castle as a set of ravenous jaws ready to devour our small capital.

It was on a dark winter afternoon that the final bills began to come in. The day-dream that had been Dacre had turned into rather an unpleasant reality. The reality that we were overdrawn at the bank If by any chance we did not like living in the castle we would not be able to escape because we could never recover what we had spent. We were enmeshed. The romantic escape-from-it-all castle had taken on the harsh substance of a prison.

Outside dusk was falling like fine ashes from a slate-grey sky. A sky so melancholy that it resembled the work of a poor art student who had not learnt the technique of scumbling. The streets were gloomy with that unattractive yellow light one often gets in London in winter. But inside our little flat it was even more gloomy.

To cheer myself up I put away the bills and began to work on my tapestry. Although I was a little worried about the scantiness of our small Georgian pieces of furniture in the vast castle rooms, I was unconcerned about covering the walls. My mother-in-law had some fine Flemish and Cluny tapestries in store, and had made us a present of them. When we visited the warehouse to collect them, we found them badly damaged where they had been folded. In fact they were in shreds.

A few years previously I had attended a London Art School where I had learnt tapestry-designing. Since then I had designed and worked a good many petit-point chair-backs and cushion-covers. So to repair these tapestries was not too hard a job, though a long one. For the two years that the architect and builders were working on the fabric of the castle I had worked on my tapestries. Now I believe that there is as much of my own stitching in them as there is original warp and weft.

That winter evening, the Cluny reds and blues of the mediaeval figures in the tapestry I was working on seemed to glow, and the tiny white flowers of the forest appeared to gleam against their verdurous background. They reminded me of the snowdrops in the boggy castle moat. The snowdrops which the children had gathered on one of our visits there. Suddenly I was no longer aware of my anxieties; only of the deep sense of security and protection conjured up by those sandstone walls set four-square to the fell winds. I felt again as I had felt that first day—that we had done the right thing. During those chaotic months I would often think of Dacre, where time was not something to race against, but to enjoy slowly. Where I would no longer have to rush from the hairdresser to my first modelling job; from work to our first cocktail party, dinner or theatre-engagement. Where Anthony would no longer have to drag himself from bed complete with hang-over to get the children to school on time before taking the tube to the city. At Dacre, I felt, time would be for living!

We spent our last six months in London in a maison-ette in Pimlico. It was on four floors with one room on each floor, and must have been converted with a herd of mountain goats in mind, rather than a human family.

I was still worried that our few precious little pieces of Chippendale and Hepplewhite might look ludicrous and lost in the vast castle rooms, when we had a stroke of luck. Three years before we had bought two land-scapes, with figures *after Watteau*, from Christies. Long after, we decided on closer inspection of our new acquisitions that two miniscule figures in the front of each picture were by the master himself, while the backgrounds were probably by a pupil. We also sus-pected that there was something a little wrong with the perspective. In spite of all this, we had the paintings restored. The restorer did a masterly job on them and sent them back complete with *Bond Street* varnish. After we had changed the heavy Victorian frames for bogus Chippendale, they looked truly magnificent. Yet we could never quite shake off the impression that there was something rather bogus about them, and consequently we put them up for resale. To our delight they fetched twice their original price. There was now £150 in the kitty with which to buy carved oak and ornate gilt for Dacre!

I began to haunt Christies, Harrods and The Pantechnicon; all my spare time was spent in hanging round auction rooms. Gradually after a little practice I learnt the tricks of the trade. Oddly enough the grandest sales yielded the best harvest. I soon discovered that prosperous Italian dealers, who usually set their sights on our type of castle furniture, seldom sat on through the lunch hour. The call of chianti and spaghetti was too strong. Then too, the well-known English dealers would refuse to lose face by bidding for antiques which were anything less than the best. By sitting on through the lunch hour, Anthony and I managed to acquire:

1 carved seventeenth century Venetian casoni—£25.

1 pair of Florentine ebony and ivory prayer-chairs with embossed leather seats—£9.

I loved these chairs, particularly the little devils in the centre of the backs, to remind the cardinals what they were praying about.

1 brass candelabra—£29.

1 carved oak sham gothic Victorian sideboard—£3.

1 enormous carved gold chair made for King George V, bearing the inscription:

This chair was used by His Majesty King George V on

the occasion of his visit to Cardiff with Queen Mary whilst the address from the corporation was being made in the City Hall, June 25th 1912.

I was nervous that the inscription would coax up the price but it did not.

We got it for £9!

Another beautiful carved oak chair incorporating a canthus leaf design cost us only £7.

The final £64 was spent on plain country oak chests and court cupboards, which over a period we managed to pick up at country sales. To complete the picture in magnificent style, Anthony's mother presented us with a lovely seventeenth century refectory table, and my mother, quite rightly thinking that no castle was complete without a tiger skin, managed to buy one through a newspaper advertisement. When Anthony is asked now where he shot it, he replies firmly: "Sloane Square."

By March 1st all the furniture was packed by Pickfords. The adventure had begun!

3 Learning the Hard Way

W<small>E</small> had exchanged our car for a Bedford van, and Anthony drove north with the back crammed with bits and pieces of luggage. This time the children and I travelled by day. The journey seemed endless, and when we arrived at Dacre the evening star was already shining over the eastern fells, silvering the mist that drifted above the sear reeds in the castle moat.

Anthony greeted me with the news that the door of our turret bedroom was too small to take our double bed and we would be sleeping in the King's Room until we could acquire two single beds. The moon rose two hours before the dawn. Through the open windows I could smell the scent which had struck me so vividly when I got off the train at Penrith. It was the scent of mountain air. But our improvised bedchamber was also fragrant with the fresias which Anthony had bought me as a house-warming present. The electricians had not yet finished their work and the room was lit by candles. It seemed vast, high, and vaulted like a church. The flickering light accentuated the massed shadows that had accumulated over the decades under the high gothic vaults. It was as though centuries of silence had been trapped between the stout beams, and embalmed there. The tapestries were already hung, and the deep blues and cluny reds glowed miraculously in the light of the flickering candles. The solid stones of the walls had taken on an amber tone. I touched them with my hands. They seemed to pulsate with life. We had given up the world, being a little tired of it in any case, and this dear beautiful fortress was all we had now. I was content.

Our first week was a chapter of accidents. I believe there was a major catastrophe on each day of the week.

Apart from the main newel staircase, there are two others which spiral almost vertically from the hall to the dungeons. On Monday Ivan fell backwards down one of these, a drop of about 20 feet. When we found him he was lying absolutely still and limp. We carried him to the van, and the whole of our first day was spent in Penrith hospital. Ivan's thick anorak must have saved him for there were no broken bones; he was merely concussed. But I had learnt my lesson! On the way home I bought padlocks and chains, and now all doors leading to the newel stairs are kept firmly locked.

Ivan was fairly immobile during Tuesday and Wednesday, but on Thursday he revived with a vengeance. Our most precious Chippendale looking-glass was lying unpacked from its crate on one of the beds. Unfortunately this was the bed on which Ivan chose to practise his karati. One of his backward somersaults ended on the mirror, and the beautiful gilt frame with its peacocks and pagodas was broken in two.

On Friday a rawlplug fell out of the stone wall and another Chippendale mirror went flying! On Saturday Ivan was right on form again. He backed into a Coromandel screen and sent it crashing into our best *after Claude* painting. Tuesday and Wednesday were not too successful either. Anthony and I spent the whole of Tuesday in unpacking and hanging paintings. By the evening we were exhausted, but decided to cheer ourselves up by lighting a log fire. Having collected some wood from our paddock we sat back to enjoy the glorious warmth. The fire was indeed glorious, the most glorious we had ever seen. Smoke and flames literally poured out of it! The builders had evidently allowed some masonry to fall down the chimney and had failed to clean it before we arrived.

On Wednesday we had the painters back with us again to repaint the blackened smoke-stained walls. The painters' arrival coincided with that of a reporter from the local paper. While we chatted with him over martinis, waxing eloquent on the quiet tranquil pleasures of country life, we all became aware of a kind of banshee howling coming from the village. I think Anthony and I realised simultaneously that Mustapha our Saluki was missing, and that someone had evidently left our gate open. Anthony was halfway down the road to Ullswater while I was still gazing in a state of numb disbelief as carcasses of hens and cascades of feathers came hurtling across the stone wall of a small rustic cottage beside Dacre Beck.

Poor Mustapha! The new and intoxicating country smells had completely gone to his head!

In the midst of the holocaust a mountainously fat woman was standing with arms akimbo. Her hair rose and fell in iron grey waves, so rigid that they might have been set in cement. Justifiably she was somewhat annoyed.

"Eh, man," she shouted when she saw Anthony. "What a scraffle! 'Im's etten eight chicks! Yon's 'im, scufterin in t'corner!"

We managed to catch Mustapha who was skulking by the midden, while she railed on: "T'auld 'un mun gie 'im a clout, or Ah'll lam 'im for ye!"

Miserably we dragged Mustapha back to the castle, and on Sunday Anthony went round to assess the damage. The cement-haired lady did not appear to have mellowed.

"'Im's etten eight Rhode Islands . . . aye, and there's udder twenty in t'back, terrible brayed. They'll nut lay fer weeks. There's twenty theer, nobbut poorly. Aye, and they'll tek no bagging. Noo git away wid ye!"

At this point Anthony, realizing with a sinking heart that these were going to be the most expensive Rhode Island Reds ever to be sold in Cumberland, offered to make good the damage. But the bargaining was not yet over, for his friend was now making for her cottage, at the same time hurling treaty terms over her shoulder.

"That's eneuf. Ah'll do nea business on a Soonda. Ah's nut fashed; sae hoot! Away wid ye!"

Eventually we paid for the eight Rhode Island Reds that Mustapha had killed, together with eggs for a whole month that the other twenty hens had refused to lay owing to being so "terrible brayed."

We had made a good beginning to country life!

We were terrified that Mustapha would have to be put down if this sort of thing happened again, and we resorted to the only possible cure. He was locked in the outhouse for twenty-four hours, with a chicken carcase tied round his neck. This horrible expedient was successful. He never killed a chicken again.

That Sunday, our seventh day in Dacre, we experienced for the first time the easterly bite of the Helm Wind. It was a savage wind which caused the willows we had just planted by the pond to lash wildly at the passing clouds, and which shrivelled their premature leaves to a rusty brown. The wind brought with it the rain which battered against the great mullioned windows like a charge of bayonets, and hurled itself against the old stone walls as if bent on their annihilation. At first we felt comfortable and cosy. We had discovered that the fireplace in the King's Room worked beautifully, even if its twin in the other room did not; the smell of the pine logs after London's smokeless fuel was pure bliss! The snugness, the warmth, the sense of solidity of the thick stone walls acted on us like a pleasant drug against the roaring storm outside. The children were for once peaceful, curled up with books, and Saki the whippet dozed on my lap. It was then that I realized that the east windows were leaking. Not just in trickles, either. Great pools were forming on the freshly-painted sills. Anthony and I tore upstairs and discovered that the same thing was happening in every room in the castle that had an east window.

All that day, as we dismally watched the angry squalls darken from silver to steel-grey as they fled from fell to fell, Anthony and I trailed round from room to room with buckets and mops. Only by nightfall did we evolve the method that we now use when storms get savage. We rolled voluminous towels along the sills and wrung them out at hourly intervals.

The windows fitted into the castle by the Earl of Sussex may have been pretty, but they will never be waterproof. Fenestration experts from all over the country have not been able to make them so.

By dawn the storm was over. The rising sun streaming through the curtainless windows reminded me of the book I had bought on how to make curtains, and of the large pile of velvet, in deep mediaeval blues and greens and Cluny reds, which was awaiting my attention. Hazily I switched on the heater for the baby's milk bottle. While I waited I watched the sun gilding the vapour that hung in the valley. A herd of glossy Fresians grazed on invisible legs. Some rays of sun spotlit the spring gorse that was growing in gold veins up the fellside. A kingfisher drew a deep blue line straight along the beck. It was as if the storm had never been.

The curtain-making was a tiring business. The windows were 15 feet high and I always like my curtains lined and interlined. Besides this there were the four young children to look after and the huge rooms to turn out. The King's Room and the Hall took me six hours each. Our nearest neighbour was a farmer who lived a short distance away in a modern cottage on the edge of the village. One day I was discussing my plight with Mrs. Wells his wife, and I think she took pity on me, for she agreed to *help me out* for two hours every morning. In no time at all the castle began to sparkle, and for those two hours I was able to finish my curtains in perfect peace. Soon they were hung beneath gold wooden pelmets decorated with the roses of Lancaster and York, which had been cut down from one of the tapestry frames. I have always preferred tapestries to hang down, flapping gently in the breeze, and considered their frame superfluous.

Summer was beginning, and now thanks to Mrs. Wells I was able to help Anthony start work on the garden. He had taken a few weeks away from work to arrange the move, and for the first time in our lives we were experiencing the glorious sensation of not being ruled by the clock. We had days without end at our service to do with as we pleased. The hours had no boundaries, and on some days we did not even bother to wind the clock at all. If we missed lunch, what did it matter? We could have a delicious high tea instead. If we had a batch of trees to plant we could abandon tea for a late dinner. For these few months the children lived on a wonderful diet of picnics and snacks. They loved it! Shopping was made incredibly easy by small travelling vans which came to the door and revealed whole grocers' shops stocked with bread, vegetables, salads and meat, down to the most exquisite delicacies such as tinned prawns and salmon. I think these vans are indigenous to this part of the country and I have never known of a time, unless the road is completely impassable with snow, when our grocer Mr. Radcliffe has not managed to get through to us somehow or other.

The grounds of the castle were composed of a six-foot high forest of briars, brambles, and elderberry bushes. Nettles and thistles were so virile in the court-yard that it was almost impossible to reach the back door.

During that first spring we were faced with the task of reclaiming the garden from an unkempt bed of weeds, and trying to make it into a thing of beauty. We spent hour after hour spraying nettles, digging-up elder roots and stabbing at docks with a solution of creosote. At the back of the castle was an acre of land which had once been a field but had now been absorbed into the desolate fell land. In time, with the aid of dock, thistle and nettle spray, and endless fertilizers, we were to turn this patch of ground into a paddock for our ponies. We were soon to learn that the conquest of our stony plot was only to be achieved by superhuman persistence. Our first willows never sprouted again after the Helm Wind had shrivelled them black, but the following year we planted more, not 'weepers' this time, but the sturdy Japanese bat variety, which now surround our pond with a fringe of soft grey green.

In our mind's eye we had laid out our little "garth"

in the style of Capability Brown. No formal flower beds for us, but clumps of trees and flowering shrubs, with lawns rolling down to the pond and the moat Fortunately when we planted the wild cherries, mountain ashes, dog roses and crab apples, all to blend with the surrounding country, we were still happily unaware of the hazards that can beset plant life if one is 600 feet above sea level. It was as well that we could not guess at the setbacks which the seasons would bring, or how for years our trees would remain obstinately stunted. We did not know then how in winter the east wind would curl our evergreens to brown scarecrows, or how, in spring, the northern gales from the Divisions would nip our apple and cherry blossom in the bud. We were unaware that in summer, two days of drought could drain the heavy clay soil to the hardness of cement, thus killing a dozen of our yews, or that the vicious premature winds of autumn, with ice in their wake, could strip our poplars and leave them a row of gaunt fish bones silhouetted against the skyline. Fortunately for us, that summer, we were full of blissful ignorance. Otherwise we might have planted nothing at all!

Beneath our new shrubberies there had once been a cobbled courtyard, but the soil deposit of three centuries had covered it with at least a foot of earth. Every time we tried to plant something our pickaxes would hit cobbles. One day while digging out the stones, I hacked into my foot by mistake, and it was while I was lying in bed recovering from a rather nasty gash that my mother sent me some press cuttings.

The *Daily Mail* had written: *Northward Ho for the Party Queen!*

The *Express*, with three pictures of my more hilarious fancy dress party outfits, asked: *Is it goodbye to all this?*

The *Evening News*, writing of Ascot, said: *Bunty's stunners will be missing from the Ascot scene. She is enjoying pastoral life in Cumberland.* Sometimes I wondered about that last sentence!

All that spring, Anthony and I continued to dig and hack at the long yellow nettle roots, and the stubborn tap-roots of the docks. Ascot seemed a million miles away. The world that those cuttings had recalled to me had been a pleasant and glamorous one, while our present life was that of a couple of peasants. Yet in those first months, the pure pleasure of plodding toil and fresh air had a narcotic affect on us, and we felt doped with the mere joy of being alive. We were absorbed, not as we had been in London by the problems of politics, economics and personalities, but by tangible things. While we worked we found a deeper consciousness of the country in which we had chosen to live. We noticed many things. The never-ending pageantry of the sky; how from Dacre Bank the vast expanse of Ullswater was diminished to a little purple pool; the yews that guarded the churchyard and the sable gloss they took on as the summer progressed. Every Cumberland churchyard has had its sentinel yews since they were used for the bows of the first borderers. Then too we would never tire of contemplating the little black powder puffs among the crowsfoot in the moat. For the first time in our lives we were using our eyes!

An interior view, Dacre Castle 1871

The same view, 1971

Photo. Eric Davidson

Our small bedroom in the East Turret

Photo. Eric Davidson

4 Enter the Animals

IT was when the third family of moorhens appeared that we acquired the first of our unusual pets. It was Amanda who found the moorhen chick lying in the rushes, with one attenuated leg quite stiff. I have heard since that sick moorhens are almost impossible to cure, but we must have had beginners' luck. We placed her in a cardboard box near the fire in a nest of hay, with a large bowl of water. She could not stand upright but managed somehow to scuttle over to the bowl of water, where she evidently felt some security. We fed her hourly on chick crumbs and finely-chopped hard-boiled egg, and in a few days her little stilt-like leg began to heal and we felt that she was sufficiently well to be nudged back to wild life. When we put her in a chicken run in the garden an extraordinary thing happened. The moorhen is usually a shy and wary bird; yet our chick's mother would daily brave two adults, four children and two dogs to visit her offspring, chattering angrily outside the wire netting, before strutting back to the reeds on her huge ungainly feet. After two weeks we rather unwillingly accepted the fact that our chick was well enough to return to the moat, so when her mother called the next morning we let her join her, and our last sight was of the little sooty ball of feathers limping in pursuit of her mother on ill-regulated gangling legs. But perhaps it was not *quite* our last sight of her, for although many of our moorhens have left us, every year a slightly lame one returns to lay her eggs in the moat and to rear at least three broods on our pond, before returning to the wilds.

Although we loved our black moorhens we could not resist an advertisement in a Sunday paper for some perching ducks, and in a moment of madness spent £10 each on a pair of Carolinas from Southern Canada and a pair of Mandarins from Eastern Asia. When the Carolinas arrived they were in their full colour, and once on the pond we were amazed by the brightness of their plumage. Their crests were greener than the opening buds of the willow herbs that fringed the pond. Their beaks were brighter than the golden gorse of spring. Their downy breast feathers were a deeper pink than the crab apple blossoms reflected beneath them in the still water. Unfortunately within five minutes we had lost the drake who had darted through the rushes and was never seen again! We ordered another Carolina drake, which arrived a week later. By this time we had sought advice as to how to keep these wild ducks on the pond. It was rather a long and tedious business. The whole family had to ring the pond and everytime the drake, completely ignoring the duck, made a dart for the rushes, we would chase him back on to the water. This process went on for two or three hours. The Mandarins were also safely installed by now, and their colours were even brighter than those of the Carolinas. They looked like two small oriental jewelled idols, floating on the still water, with wide-spread crests of emerald, wings of amber, and breast feathers of amethyst.

We were delighted with our new pets, but as spring wore on to summer the ducks began to grow restless;

the call of running water was strong in them. Our castle was built on a spur of land, a strategic point where the Dacre Beck joins the River Eamont. This means water from the hills, and everywhere about us were streams running gaily and freely beside the low stone walls, down the fell sides. It was no wonder that we could not keep our wild ducks. For two months they were faithful to their little pond, but with the start of the mating season we began to dread the sound of the telephone when kind neighbours would ring to enquire:

"Is it yer ducks a-hint of Dalemain on t'Eamont?"
Or:
"Them ducks au awa among t'mallards on t'beck."
And:
"Them auld birds o' yours up yond be under t'bench, a-baggin' t'turkey pellets."

Anthony had learnt his walking in a harder school than me. He had escaped from a prison camp in Italy and walked through enemy territory from Parma to Florence to join the allied forces. So although he now had a pathological dislike for long walks unless he was shooting or coursing, he was a good deal faster than me. He would generally track down our ducks after walking over about six miles of fell and mountain, while I was still a few miles back stuck on a barbed-wire fence. Anthony's technique for catching these wild little birds was fairly simple. He would stalk them furtively and then hurl a handkerchief or jumper or anything that came to hand the last few yards, and if it succeeded in covering them, they would remain completely quiet and still under this comfortingly dark pall, literally asking to be caught. However, after about three months our ducks were playing truant more and more often, so when they were reported absent in July we did not immediately bother to investigate. After five days we did become worried, and began to comb the country. At this time we had not yet become inured to the unfortunate ends which most of our pets were to meet, and when we found our ducks lying on the fellside with their heads and necks missing, we were shattered. For a long time we had been worried about a predatory wild cat that roamed the district, but this decapitation of its victim was undoubtedly the work of a fox. We blamed ourselves bitterly for not having tried to find our ducks before. Now it was too late. The bright plumage of the little birds had already faded to a dusty brown and they were now no more than bundles of claws and tattered feathers. That afternoon we buried them in the corner of the pond field, under the sapling of a weeping beech.

When Anthony was in the Long Range Desert Group he was presented with his first Saluki by a Bedouin. The Arabs, whose barren land has been the nursery of so many civilizations, have also provided the world with two perfect creatures—their intelligent and docile horses, and their elegant and graceful gazelle hounds, or Salukis, the oldest sporting dogs in the world.

From the day that these hounds are born, they are brought up in the sheik's tent with his own children, and treated with the same kindness and consideration. "This is not a dog," say the Arabs, "it is a Saluki and Barake—specially blessed." In the desert these hounds are so cherished and loved by their owners that they are never sold; only given away to a friend as a token of honour and respect.

After the war Anthony took his first Mustapha to Germany, where he used him for hunting roedeer, but soon he had to leave for England. A Saluki pines in captivity away from human companionship, so instead of putting him into quarantine Anthony gave him away. He found a very happy home with a daughter of a French duke, with a groom specially detailed to look after him!

Anthony's second Saluki, who was also called Mustapha, we bought in England. He was three years old by the time we came to Cumberland. I think he was without doubt the most beautiful dog I have ever seen. His coat, the colour of pale desert sand, feathered into white at his tail, his forelegs, and the back of his thighs. The tasselled ears were whitish too. His eyes were dark, deep, gentle and poignant. His movements were as smooth as silk. His whole appearance gave an impression of elegance, symmetry and nobility.

We bought a life insurance for Mustapha in the form of a Swaledale orphan. Swaledales are black-faced sheep, now out of fashion in the dales but usually found on the fells. We punched a large hole in the teat of one of Sebastian's bottles and gave our lamb four full bottles of milk a day. This was not nearly such a tedious business as it sounds, for Edward—as our little ram was called—would drink his bottle in about 30 seconds. My own children, I recalled, had usually taken at least twenty minutes! Mustapha and Edward took to each other immediately and we now felt that our Saluki was at least 95 per cent sheep-proof. Of course with a coursing dog there is always the imponderable 5 per cent!

September came and we were still digging and hacking at the elder roots embedded deep in the walls of the castle, but when two Romany friends came to call on us with their coursing dogs, we decided to take

a break and give Mustapha an afternoon on the fells.
We all piled into the van. Ned of High Burnthwaite—
I don't think we ever knew his surname—had his
lurcher Cassius, and Jeff Brown brought his fine old
greyhound bitch. We stopped the car at the eastern end
of Ullswater and followed the grass-grown track that
was once a Roman road, up to Tarn Moor. In the
distance we could hear the slow thudding of the engines
of the *Lady of the Lakes*, as the old steamer ploughed
slowly across the lake to Hightown Harbour. Now the
path forded a little stream and a hundred yards on, after
climbing a dry-stone wall, we found ourselves on the
heathery wastes of White Stone Moor. Now the sound
of the ship's engines had faded behind us and we were
alone in the silence of the moor with the falcons, the
peeweets and the hares.

The men walked on ahead with long unhurried steps,
speaking seldom. Cassius and Mustapha were seeking
their own trails and hunting alone. Mustapha with his
hare feet was finding the going easy. His was an ideal
build for the fells with his light sinuous body. He was
a fine stayer and a good jumper. As they walked along
the men noted the holes in the dry-stone walls that
would take the hares to safety, and where the cover lay
in the russet bracken. Strictly speaking we were
poachers. The land we were approaching had been
bought by Manchester Water Board and was now
common land, but the sporting rights belonged to one
or two large landowners in the district. We were
perfectly within our rights to walk our dogs across the
fell, but if they put up a hare, we were breaking the
law. In Romany eyes, however, laws are made to be
broken. And was there not Nature's more inexorable
law to be taken into account? It is not possible to quell

the hunting and killing instinct of a hound, and perhaps it would be cruel to try. It was borne in upon me as we walked over the rusty bracken of the silent fell, that here was a world as old as history itself, a world that had stood still for two thousand years. A hare started up from some bracken and fled towards a ragged wind-blown fir wood. Mustapha made a *cate* endways of the lurcher. Before it reached its sanctuary, Cassius' jaws had snapped its backbone asunder. Mustapha's first kill was in a grassy field by High Weind, a ruined moss-grown farm. But now an odd thing happened. Unlike the lurcher and the greyhound, Mustapha did not spring upon his kill. He completely ignored it and came with his easy, dignified camel walk straight back to his master. Anthony told me later that Mustapha, like his first Saluki, seldom killed to eat. He hunted for the sheer pleasure of it.

It was this autumn that for the first time in my life a dream came true. When I was fourteen years old I had spent three years with an Irish aunt and uncle who ran racing stables on the Curragh, together with a stud farm. Much to my joy after a six-month apprenticeship on a fat brown cob, I was allowed to exercise the race horses and ride the gallops. Ever since that time I had longed for a horse of my own.

In London, after we had bought Dacre Castle, I began to have a recurrent dream. We were in a region where silver-green fells cut frescoes in the dark sky and red deer made lordly silhouettes against their peaked edges. But Anthony and I and all the children were riding rough ponies over boggy patches of white moss, clumps of spiky rushes, and slipping stones. I remember in my dreams being seized with an icy terror lest we should not be able to leave the mere and gain the heights. But suddenly—for this was a dream—we were galloping over the springy thyme-speckled turf at the summit of the fell, all neck and neck, with the smell of leather and horse-sweat and heather-blown wind, straight into a world of unimagined rapture. That first autumn we experienced this dream in reality. We now had horses!

Anthony had a large fell pony, the type which in days gone by had carried 16 stones of lead for the mines up and down the fellside and which now carried his 12 stones with ease. He bought him from Mr. Allen, a hill farmer from Park Foot, who had bred him himself and had just broken him in. At that time he was four. Now, as Anthony never tires of telling us, he is the handy hunter champion of Penrith! His name was Saladin. I had a hybrid blood mare—not the shaggy pony of my dream—called Sheba. For Amanda we bought an Irish potter's pony, a bay which on arrival, owing to poor feeding, appeared to be extremely docile, but which through the years has developed into one of the most fiendish and capricious ponies I have ever known. However Amanda loves him, and calls him Leprechaun.

We could not keep our horses and ponies at home for we were unable to rent land. In Dacre the farmers count every blade of grass! We eventually found grazing for them at the foot of Barton Fell on a caravan site on the south side of Ullswater. This suits Leprechaun, the Irish gypsy pony, extremely well, for he is forever leaping out of his field and emptying the caravanners' dustbins for a whole mile around! It is from here that we ride, climbing the 1,300 feet to the summit of the fells.

In nearly every respect my dream has come true. Up on the wild ridges of Barton Fell are red deer, their carriage and gait a thing of unutterable beauty, their spread of horn like something out of ancient times. Even the squelchy patches in my dream have come true. Lovely little yellow flowers like stars grow amongst the sinister pale sphagnum moss. These areas have never proved dangerous for Saladin, the sure-footed one. But they have been tiresome for Sheba, with her fine legs and small hooves, and for Leprechaun, when Amanda was only nine. I remember she cried after her fall, but her love of riding survived the trauma. Something peculiar happens to a horse when it falls into a bog. It seems to give in and cease to struggle. It usually takes our combined efforts to yank it out. I think we have now marked all the dangerous bogs within a ten-mile radius of where we ride, but we often see children straggling behind one of the numerous pony treks that depart from the shores of Ullswater, and this is something that worries us very much.

It was a day in late November. The sky was dull-grey. Ullswater was a placid dream. It was then that we saw the white hare.

Mustapha, whose trailing faculties had been greatly developed, put it up in a narrow gully, a shadowy apparition against the grey scree. Anthony immediately called him off, not wanting him to kill such an unusual animal. The hare sped with ghostly fleetness into the twisted tangle of hawthorn at the foot of the rocky face. But not before we had taken in every detail of this strange creature.

It was not a blue or mountain hare; not a polar or Greenland hare that turns white in winter. This was a brown hare that had been born an albino. Mustapha's jaws dripped with hot desire. But he stopped in his tracks, obedient to his master's command.

However, one bleak December afternoon he took his prey. The white hare had bounded at a tangent straight across his path. It was too late for Anthony to stop him. The great hare was away over the short bare springy heather, bounding across the sharp points of *junctus actus*. The course lasted two miles, with twenty turns of the hare, but murder followed close. There was a stark element of dramatic correctness in the kill of the white hare, by the white dog, on the bare grey screes of White Stone Moor.

During the last five years we have seen three more of these albino hares. We were sad about the death of Mustapha's hare. But the death of our Saluki, when it came, seemed to us more heart-breaking than that of his victim!

5 *The Sad Winter*

Wᴇ were worried by the coming of winter for the sake of our newly-planted trees and shrubs. Day after day a cold vapour lay over the valley of Dacre village, and rimmed the withered *ladies' garters* and dwarf willows which we had planted round the pond. For days the rushes in the moat were white with mist, and the horses' drinking trough was filmed with brittle ice which had to be broken every morning. For weeks a dull anaemic sun without warmth or colour lay over the fells. Then in its place came the east wind bringing hail and sleet. Three nights before Christmas the hail turned to a fine powdery snow that whirled out of the starless sky, settling nowhere. But by Christmas Eve the flakes had become thicker and accumulated in still, pallid drifts on the castle battlements.

We were excited at the thought of our first Christmas in the country. The setting seemed so exactly right. We gathered holly and mistletoe and made brightly coloured pomander balls. We decorated every room with holly, fir cones and branches that glittered in gold and silver. I hate to buy Norwegian spruce that have their roots dipped in turpentine, so on this occasion we had cheated a little and bought a beautiful blue cedar, which in my mind's eye I already saw as a forest giant looking silvery and glossy against the castle's pale mauve stone walls.

I remember how we lit the red candles of our brass chimes and settled down amongst the usual Christmas Eve chaos of paper and string. We were all feeling blissfully happy and at peace with the world. The children and I were re-dressing some little nativity dolls which I had made eight years previously for Amanda's first Christmas. These were to be placed in our trefoil font. Amanda had made a star of Bethlehem to hang over them.

I had only one worry on my mind. We had erected some close-boarding six feet in height so that we could exercise Mustapha when we could not take him for walks, but latterly he had learnt to jump this, for there was a sheep dog bitch, or *cur* as they are called in these parts, on the neighbouring farm, and Mustapha was taking a passionate interest in her. But I was not greatly concerned, for I knew Mustapha would not wander any further. The attraction of the sheep dog was too strong. Now he had his great length stretched along the hearth-rug, his long muzzle resting near Anthony's feet, his soft brown eyes gazing at his master's face. There was no hint that he aimed to stray.

I had just finished making Mary's blue mantle when Anthony said: "Where's Mustapha?"

I looked at the hearth-rug. He had gone. "The door to the newel stairs must have blown open in a gust of wind," I said.

We did not really panic for we had worried so often before and been reassured and made to feel foolish when, time after time, we had found Mustapha trotting happily back from the farm buildings where his lady-friend lived. But that night for some reason the feeling of unease came more strongly. With a strained feeling of fright I hurried to the farm. Anthony ran up the bankside from where he could see the flock of sheep grazing calmly. Of course I found the renegade in his usual place outside the locked stable door. Our devotion to Mustapha had as usual exaggerated our fears!

We had just piled the last cotton-wool ball on the Christmas tree when the telephone rang. The man on the other end of the line spoke for about a minute and his voice sounded pleasant and cultured; but from Anthony's tone which had become very stiff and polite, I knew that some sort of disaster had occurred. When he put down the receiver he immediately fetched his coat and went out, merely saying: "A sheep's been killed. Colonel D's farm manager thinks it's Mustapha."

Mustapha tried to follow his master, wagging his feathery tail in expectation of a walk, but I held him back. Then I sat by the fire gazing into the flames, and waited. I felt desperately frightened, for I knew that if the case was proved against Mustapha, he would have to be put down. I felt enraged too that this circumstance which we had so carefully guarded against, should have actually materialized.

When Anthony came back he told me that he had had interviews with the landowner and his farmer. A sheep had apparently run into some barbed wire and bled to death. Mustapha had been seen near the farm. Anthony had explained that Mustapha was sheep-proof, but of course the answer was inevitable and also justified: "Yes, but the dog was on my land."

We had always realized that keeping a Saluki in sheep-farming country was rather like playing chess against a Grand Master when your Queen and two Bishops have been confiscated at the start. We had agreed that if there was ever any trouble over sheep-worrying there could be only one answer.

Guilty or innocent? It was immaterial! Once your dog is mentioned in the same breath as someone else's sheep, it is finished. Farmers lose thousands of pounds each year through the damage done by dogs, and in some parts of the country they have even had to give up farming altogether.

A week after Christmas, Anthony took Mustapha to Penrith, but it was not until a year afterwards that he told me what had happened. There had been some big football match in the neighbourhood and the streets were crowded with cheerful people wearing coloured scarves and rosettes and shouting slogans. The vet was out but his secretary said that he would return in half an hour. Anthony left the dogs in the van and for thirty haunted minutes wandered from pub to pub drinking whiskies. When he returned to the surgery the vet was waiting and Anthony explained that he wanted Mustapha destroyed. Like most of his profession, the vet was a compassionate man and when Anthony went out to the van to collect Mustapha he followed him. Saki leapt out as soon as the door was opened, but for once Mustapha held back. Angrily Anthony called Saki, who was investigating the wheel of a nearby car. When he got him back into the van the vet was holding Mustapha's lead. Anthony hurried round the front of the car to the driving seat and did not look back . . .

Our first winter in Dacre stands out with a terrible clarity in my mind. We had just lost Mustapha, and by some unhappy coincidence we were to lose Saki a month later.

Anthony and a friend of ours, John Strutt, had taken Saki coursing on the fells. I knew they usually walked about 15 miles on these occasions but they were generally home by 6 o'clock.

On the 25th of January I had cooked the dinner by seven o'clock and lit the candles in their pewter sticks on the dinner table, for the men were usually hungry after a day in the open air. The curtains were not drawn for we loved to watch the pageant of the sky through the large mullion *Bess of Hardwick* windows. Above the horizon of hills a furious sky tore in sweeping companies of cumulus clouds from the Divisions, across Ullswater, to White Stone Moor. But everything in the room looked cosy and shining. I had polished the refectory table in readiness for our small dinner party and there was a pot roast simmering in the oven.

By 8 o'clock the black shapes in the sky against the moor were vast and threatening. The wind was racing over Ullswater and up the fellside, driving with it sheets of rain. I began to feel an odd anxiety and rest-lessness. I tried to work on a tapestry I had designed, depicting Mustapha and the white hare. But it was no good. I could only listen to the wind whistling round the turrets and the rain battling against the windows. By 10 o'clock my panic was growing. The knocker banged. When I opened the door John and Anthony looked grave and worried. Saki was not with them, and I immediately knew that some sort of disaster had taken place out there on the fells. The story did not take long to tell.

The blizzard had come swiftly out of the dusk, and if Saki had not just put up a hare they would have noted the threatening signs of cloud and wind and taken shelter. But already it was too late. Saki had left the dead bracken and flat moss of White Stone Moor far behind. Beyond three dry-stone walls which our little London-reared whippet had leapt with ease, was a vast wind-blown fir wood, and here Anthony and John had

lost him. In High Weind young pheasants were reared,
and I knew we were all thinking the same thing . . .
here in this wood gins would be set for their enemies.

By midnight the storm had succumbed to a grey
mist, and there was a full moon. I arranged for a baby-
sitter and we hunted for Saki for two hours across
White Stone Moor and High Weind, where Saki had
last been seen. We walked three abreast with about
thirty yards between us, calling his name at intervals,
but from the black humps of the hills came only the
echo of our voices and . . . silence.

By 8 o'clock the next morning we were again on the
high cold moorland, and so we were every other day
that week. Although we had now combed every inch
of the wood, the thought of traps was still in our minds.
All that week I could not help remembering Saki as he
had been in London. He had belonged to my little girl
Amanda, and even playing in Kensington Gardens he
had never once let her out of his sight. I will never forget
that anxious little whippet face searching for her among
the swings and roundabouts. I was surprised by the
attitude of some farm workers, of whom we made
enquiries. They were sympathetic enough when they
told us they had not seen our dog—but their first
question was always the same: "Is she valuable?"

After 24 hours we advertised in the local paper,
offering a reward, but it was not until two weeks had
passed that we heard any news.

The man's voice on the telephone sounded gruff and
dour, but his first words made my heart leap with joy:

"Well, y've bin lucky. I hev yer laal dog aback o'
High Weind." My effusive thanks were soon cut short.

"Na, na, 'e's nut alive; 'e must've brok 'is back or
summat o't sooart. Will ye be gaan to tek 'im yam?"

The telephone was near Amanda's bedroom, where she was already tucked up for the night. I knew that I had conveyed nothing of the news of Saki's death in words, but from the tone of my voice she must have guessed, for as I put down the receiver I could hear her sobbing into her pillow.

Mr. C. who had telephoned us was a fell farmer, a tenant of High Weind. When we found him he was busy with his work, but somewhat reluctantly he gave us some vague instructions as to where we could find Saki's body.

High up on White Stone Moor we could see Ullswater, nestling curdled grey against banks of vapour. Across the lake the castle stood out like bleached bone on the bleak horizon. The little corpse lay by a boundary stone, on a piece of land that I am sure we had combed. So our little Kensington-bred whippet had met his end amongst these quiet fells while coursing a hare. Evidently he had broken his back on the boundary stone. He had crashed into an obstacle as so many greyhounds are wont to do because his head was down and the light failing. Or had he? This was something we would never know. Saki was only four, and we had loved him dearly since he was a tiny nervous puppy.

On the cold fellside we wrapped him in an old cot blanket and carried him to the van, which Anthony had managed to drive up the bumpy Roman road that ended about a mile away. We buried him at home under the weeping beech. For some days we could hardly bear to be in the castle where Saki had so often cuddled up with Amanda and me under a rug, while we watched television in the evenings. Nor could I bear the garden, where a small blue whippet seemed to be forever waiting for us to take him for a walk with one paw raised and an anxious, worried, expectant look on his face.

In the spring, to cheer ourselves up, we decided to invest in some pigeons, and applied for a pair of garden fantails through one of our favourite papers *Exchange and Mart*. We had kept some of these delightful birds in London and had always liked them. We found them peaceful and unpredatory, faithful to their mates, loving parents and affectionate to one another. Unfortunately when our first beautiful fantails arrived we still had some builders with us. The rains of early spring had churned the garden to a quagmire and we were having some gravel laid for a drive. Anthony had found a perfect room for the pigeons on the top of one of the turrets and we intended to keep them immured there for two or three weeks until they considered it home. After wiring up the turret window we released the pigeons from their box and they fluttered on to the little straw nest we had made for them, and sat cooing contentedly. Anthony and I then went down to inspect our new drive. The young builder who had just finished laying it had disappeared. We were just in time to see our two pigeons preening themselves on the window sills in the warm March sunshine before soaring above the battlements and winging away into the distance beyond the Divisions. How on earth, we wondered, had they knocked down their wire? It just didn't seem possible. It wasn't! The workman who had considered himself a pigeon-fancier had objected to seeing pigeons shut up and had let them free. Poor pigeons! They had come straight from Birmingham and I often wondered if they ever managed to adapt themselves to country life and find another home.

Our next effort to buy pigeons through *Exchange and*

Mart was no more fortunate. Instead of two white garden fantails arriving, we opened the cardboard box to discover six rather unattractive liver and white wild pigeons. These we let go immediately.

Third time lucky . . . or were we? Our final order through *Exchange and Mart* was a success, and after the pigeons had spent three weeks in their turret we let them out. With our hearts in our mouths we watched the two snow-white birds soar twice about the turrets, then drop down again out of the sky to their little sill and pop into their turret room, where they began to settle down to a peaceful and domestic existence— almost too domestic as it turned out. Within two years we had about a hundred pigeons, and within three, in spite of all our efforts to keep the numbers down, we had two hundred! Kind neighbours suggested that we should go up to the turret to collect the eggs. Alas it was too late. Over sixty refugee pigeons had flown off to higher and more inaccessible turrets, which through the centuries have somehow lost their stairs and now would only be accessible to a trapeze artist. Irate farmers in the near vicinity who saw our birds descending in white clouds upon their grain merely suggested that we shoot the whole lot! Yet this we could not bring ourselves to do. The birds were so charming and friendly, allowing the children to fondle and pet them, even perching on their hands like falcons without jesses. The situation was not helped by the constant stream of racing pigeons which joined us at weekends and stayed on as unwelcome guests devouring our own birds' corn and maize and wheat, and producing clever, wily, but rather unattractive patchwork babies. Eventually Anthony hung a bosun's chair over the parapets and cleared out the turrets, wiring them against subsequent marauders. Just lately the pigeon situation is definitely looking up, for we have now found a good home for all our surplus birds in a wild-life park that has just opened a few miles away.

After paying for the drive and the close-boarding fence for Mustapha, there was positively no money left in the kitty, so during that second spring, Anthony and I began to clear the piles of debris left by the builders and by previous tenants of the castle. One of these tenants had been a nursery gardener from Glasgow, whose wife had evidently insisted on hurling all her cans straight out of the window. This had been at least ten years earlier, but the rubbish had never been removed. Apart from the tins, there were parts of old cars and tractors, old bedsprings, and some intriguing ancient farm implements. We rather hoped these might be museum pieces but they turned out to be worthless. We also found some interesting-looking bones in the moat, which we imagined might have belonged to one of the early Dacres, but a lady doctor to whom we showed them could not identify them. Fortunately though, she was married to a vet who told us that they belonged to a horse. After we had loaded the van six or seven times and driven it to a rubbish dump, we gave up and turned the rest of the pile of tins into a rock garden. It looked pretty for a while, but the small plants were soon eaten by our bantams and peacocks.

6 *Spring is a Peacock*

For two months of that second spring the rain dripped, drizzled, spat or simply poured. Water gushed through the windows, under the doors and down the big open chimneys. Damp crept into the webbing of the sheets giving them the feel of clammy seaweed. Because of our hurry to move into the castle, the plaster had been put on to the stone walls before they had sufficiently dried out. Then paint had been added to the plaster before it had dried out. We were off to a bad start. Now, thanks to the rain, most of our walls were growing some interesting mushrooms and toadstools. Owing to the fact that there was no more Kinsman lolly, painters had become a thing of the past and Anthony and I had already repainted and damp-proofed most of the rooms in the castle at least twice. One turret bathroom had been repainted four times until, in desperation, we decided to lay tiles. I might have ignored the mushrooms until Sebastian, our year-old baby, needed a little less care, but in a few weeks we would once more be open to the public, and stately homes are meant to be stately.

On the 30th of April I tried to sleep to the dismal lullaby of *pitter patter pitter patter*, so tired after painting ceilings from high ladders that I ached in every bone. "Is it worth it?" I kept thinking. My beautiful castle was turning into a *triffid*. The wretched rain had begun to drip through the roof. A school had come to visit us the previous summer, and against their masters' instructions, 80 horrid little St. Trinian fiends had clambered over our precious slates. After appearing so pretty at the start, the castle was beginning to look dilapidated again. Everything that spring seemed to conspire against us. Ancient dust, probably a hundred years old, was beginning to seep through the new floor boards. The children were constantly trampling thick clay into the house. Mice would come to the table and nibble at the food when I was not looking, and to crown it all the bats were back! Yet before the summer season somehow —*somehow* the place must look immaculate again!

But as a pretty rippling pink dawn was breaking over the eastern fells on the 1st of May, everything came right again. I awoke aching and grumpy, thinking of my unfinished ceiling, when the telephone began to ring. It was the kind old fell farmer who rented me grazing for my mare Sheba. Sheba had obligingly had a foal. Neither the dealer who sold me Sheba, nor I, had suspected such an event when I bought her, so we now had two for the price of one! But it was not just this that made me happy. When I saw the little foal for the first time, on his long wobbly legs, with his fluffy bay coat and soft velvet nose, I realized that spring had really come at last. Even in this sunless hollow of White Stone Fell, usually so full of dark shadow, the fronds of bracken were beginning to rear heraldic heads, and the shores of Ullswater were veined with golden gorse.

We called the foal Nimrod, which means *the bold hunter*. He was not really particularly bold. Indeed he was rather a timid little thing. We just liked the name.

By the middle of May the painting was done and we once more began to work like mad upon the garden.

The previous spring we had planted a tiny orchard and some of the apple trees were bravely blossoming amongst an invading army of elders. How I hated those elders! Over the years they have become one of the major obsessions of my life. They drag all the goodness from the soil, produce hundreds of saplings if our backs are turned for a moment, and even sprout from the castle walls. We have always had to dig and hack these monsters out by the roots, as we dare not use sodium chlorate because of the animals.

That spring we planted wistaria and clematis where the elders had been on the south wall, together with a rowan beneath the children's bedroom window. The rowan was only three feet high, but I could already imagine its lovely scarlet berries tapping against the mullion panes. At this time the castle was surrounded by a concentration-camp-type fence which consisted of sheep wire topped with barbed wire to keep out the huge fresians which were always ready to plunder and pillage our garden. To soften the Belsen look, Anthony and I attempted to hack through the cobbles and plant a cypress hedge. But the stones were so closely packed that the *lawsonianas* stayed rusty brown for at least three years, although now I am happy to say that the little trees have turned a glossy dark green. They have at last managed to thrust their roots through the cobbles, and are flourishing.

As well as our constant struggle against the wilderness that was forever invading our garden, we were also kept extremely busy with the animals which we seemed to be acquiring in alarming quantities. It was never safe to throw out any odd cardboard box found lying about the house, for it usually contained fledglings which had fallen from their nests and were being fed on hard-boiled egg and chick crumbs. There would also occasionally be baby chickens, or worse still mice. Our chickens were extremely pretty. They were Old English game bantams, blue, red and silver duck wing cockerels which strutted and crowed about the garden with their harems of partridge hens scratching up the flower beds. In the winter though, our bantam cocks, like most of our other animals and birds, ignored the garden and hovered around the front door all day long, trying to invade the hall. When they were chased out they would let out furious squawks, and assume an indignant mien. Unlike other people who keep hens, we seldom seem to have any eggs. Game bantams are very much more intelligent than ordinary hens and consequently much more clever at concealing their eggs. We sometimes find them hidden under the *golden rain* in the front flower bed, tucked behind the hay, and even once in the van. But never, never in their nesting boxes. The bantams live in the garage, where they have been joined by some of our surplus pigeons. These pigeons, which are extremely motherly, often insist on sitting on the bantam eggs. This only adds to the confusion. Over the years, these caches of hidden eggs have turned into 30 or 40 baby bantams which have subsequently become full-grown birds. As in the case of the pigeons, we cannot bear to kill them, so our grain bill has soared.

Sapphia's pony Pixie, and Ivan's donkey Columbine are also much too friendly. Pixie was once brought indoors for Sapphia's birthday party, when she proceeded to devour the cake and candles in two seconds flat, and ever since that unfortunate day she has insisted on galloping up the steps and charging the door whenever she thinks there is something cooking, or when she smells chocolate. Columbine too has proved rather a failure. We had read of a quiet 'darling' donkey for sale in the local paper, and had rushed off hot-foot. Although quiet enough when the children tried her out at her home near the Roman Wall at Brampton, once back at Dacre she began to behave like the wildest bucking bronco ever seen in a rodeo show. The only children she would tolerate on her back were Ivan and Sebastian who were both under three. Her maternal instinct was strong and she was kind with the little ones, but as soon as any of our children imagined that they could ride, and mistakenly tried to guide her, she would plunge and buck and throw them off her back. In the case of Ivan she broke his nerve for riding for at least a year. A delightful little cart painted bright green and red had come with Columbine, complete with a miniature carthorse harness, but this she adamantly refused to pull. We had been in love with the idea of owning a donkey, and Columbine was certainly beautiful. She was small and brown with melting doe-like eyes, and a passion for dogs. Once in the early days when poor Mustapha had to be beaten with a rolled-up newspaper for taking an interest in a sheep, she let out a long bray, more like a cry of anguish, and trotted over to lick his face. After three years, when she had finally thrown off Sebastian a dozen times, disillusion with Columbine became final. However, we kept her on solely for decoration, and for any friends, with children under three, who came to stay with us!

When Sapphia was seven, we bought Pixie from a local farmer. She was an undistinguished-looking Welsh pony with a coat of a soggy dun colour, but apart from a rather unpleasant habit of giving me unexpected bites on the behind while I was saddling her, she was a perfect pony in every way. Strangely enough she never had a *go* at her little mistress. The pair seemed to have an affinity. Now that we had Columbine, Pixie and Edward the ram in our small paddock, we had to do a good deal of dung-collecting to keep the land free from worms. This was a fairly exhausting job, but of course splendid for the roses.

The landscape in front of the castle was tapestried with sheep, and dog roses in bloom. We noticed that the sheep had just been clipped. This reminded us that Edward too should now be relieved of his thick hot fleece. Mr. Wells our farmer friend kindly helped us out. He clipped our ram with old-fashioned shears rather than a machine. The result was extremely smart. Then we had a seven pound fleece on our hands and not a clue what to do with it. Until I had a brainwave . . .

Hurrah! My Christmas present problem was solved! The fleece must be spun and knitted into jumpers for our entire family. Just imagine Christmas presents from our own pet lamb! I had read in the local paper of a woman in Wattadale who collected the fluff from sheep's coats out of the hedgerows and spun them into wool. So why not our gorgeous fleece?

We eventually located Mrs. Tirral who lived in a prim white house surrounded by a prim white fence. Inside were hundreds of white plastic doyleys and white antimacassars, and Mrs. Tirral herself had on a lovely white starched apron. In the centre of the room, in pride of place, was the spinning wheel which Mrs. Tirral told us was a hundred years old.

She agreed to spin our wool and even gave us all a lesson in spinning. It was not at all easy. A few weeks later she rang up to say that she had spun the fleece into skeins. She had washed it first but had not removed all the natural oils as these would help to keep the cold out. She hoped we were pleased.

And we *were* pleased! There it was, piles and piles of lovely natural-coloured wool with an occasional black thread running through it. It was very unusual. The only thing to be done now was to knit it up!

The socks which I knitted for Anthony could have stood up on their own, and the jumpers felt like barbed wire. But one thing was certain—they would never wear out!

Now that we had cleared the rubbish from the grounds and got a lawn going, our minds immediately turned to peacocks. In the Earl of Sussex's day a peacock would have cost £1,000, but now it appeared we could buy one for £10.

The reason for our six month old cock being sold was rather a sad one. Our older children had started school at Hartland Hall, a little private school about three miles away. From the outside, the stone house looked rather like *Wuthering Heights*, but inside it had a delightfully friendly and cosy atmosphere.

Miss Evans the head-mistress, who was an artistic and imaginative woman, had been keeping peafowl for two years, but during her most recent holiday period she had let the house to a youth club, and her favourite hen had been stoned to death by some of the boys, while sitting on its eggs. This not unnaturally broke Miss Evans' spirit and she decided to get rid of all her birds. There was also another reason for this decision which we did not hear until later. The school gardener had announced that either the birds left or he did!

After we had arranged to buy one of Miss Evans' cocks, we began to work on an old chicken house, where he was to be shut up for two weeks. We put new chicken wire along the front and a wooden perch about six feet above the ground, as peafowl are extremely susceptible to damp. Then we disinfected and white-washed the whole place.

When Anthony brought the long cardboard box home from school we laid it carefully outside the wired pen. It looked unnaturally still and I wondered if the jolting of the van had killed the bird. Excitedly the children had begun to untie the knots of string, when the box suddenly burst open and a little crowned head shot out with a white suede face above a brilliant blue serpentine neck. That was all that I could take in before the young cock soared high above the battlements and then down—down—straight down wind. The last sight we had of him was over the Divisions and the new plantation of a hundred thousand firs. Ivan, Sapphia and Sebastian all began to cry simultaneously. It was evident that our peacock had gone for ever.

Again we advertised, and again to no avail. We waited two weeks and then ordered another peacock. This time we were careful not to untie the box until it was safely in the pen. Although only five months old, this was already a beautiful bird with dark bold liquid eyes. Of course his tail would not grow for at least eighteen months. We fed him on corn, flaked maize and turkey-rearing pellets, and he seemed extremely contented. A week later Mrs. Wells arrived with some astonishing news. A farmer on the Divisions had told her that a strange little turkey was "baggin'" his hen's corn. We telephoned immediately, and the next day an ancient car rattled down the drive driven by a man with a small boy beside him holding our peacock. The pea-cock, which in India is reputed to be fierce enough to attack a grown man and tear out his eyes, was tucked nonchalantly under the little boy's arm.

So now we had Romeo—as our Hartland Hall peacock

was called—and another nameless peacock in the pen. Clearly we would have to find a Juliet, and yet another bride. The peahens, when they arrived, were as pretty as the cocks, though in a more subdued key. Their moss-green necks were tinged with primrose, fading into speckled fawn and white, and their little faces emphasized mysterious dark eyes, like those of an Indian woman, with kohl at the corners.

After a few weeks we let them out of their pen, but again the two cocks sailed away beyond the horizon with the hens in hot pursuit. At this time we only had a few bantams, and our peafowl seemed to be drawn as if by a magnet to all the chicken farms in the district. Fortunately most of the farmers were friendly and extremely honest people, and were kind enough to return our birds to us. In fact I believe one man became so involved in the tantalizing task of chasing Romeo from tree to tree, that he abandoned his hay harvest for at least three days.

When we were at last back to full strength we struck on a brilliant idea. We had noticed how previously our two peacocks had been rather attracted to our Bedford van. It was black, and although usually rather muddy it was just possible for them to see their reflection in it. I never discovered if this was mere vanity, or whether the cocks saw in the painted surface a rival for their wives' affections. In any case they obviously found the whole thing fascinating; if a dusty van could give them such amusement, why not a lovely gleaming mirror?

The experiment was a wild success! The two cocks jostled each other to get a good view of themselves, and now I became convinced that the reason for their interest was vanity, and not jealousy of an interloper. The hens took little interest in the mirror, but evidently if their men were happy, so too were they. Now they scarcely ever left us—or if they did it was only to investigate some succulent spring lettuces in the village gardens. But as they were always chased off by justifiably irate ladies with brooms in their hands, they always came winging back like homing pigeons. Except, of course, that at the same time they were invariably screaming at the tops of their voices.

7 Rateable Value

Summer was now in full swing. There were marsh marigolds in the copses and gorse was turning the fell-sides gold. The buds of the old ash tree in our garden, sulky for so long, had opened at last, and among the *water crowsfoot* in the moat we had about five families of baby moorhens.

We were now conducting a number of large parties round the castle, mainly from ladies' guilds and institutes. All our visitors have, without exception, been charming, appreciative and very interested. But how I am longing for the fashion for Louis Quinze shoes to reach Penrith! Stiletto heels are still high fashion here, and our beautiful American pine floors are already ruined with the pock marks left by their lethal steel tips. Not long ago we had a party of 45 archaeologists, which was extremely unnerving as I felt that they could tell me a great deal more about the castle than I could tell them.

One morning in late summer we had to prepare ourselves to show round two officers from the department of rates and taxes. When we moved into Dacre Castle, one of the things that had charmed us about it was its rateable value. Owing to the poor condition of the building, it was assessed as a ground floor flat with rates of £29.

Immediately, Anthony and I were thrown into a quandary. Should we give the civil servants drink to make them feel friendly and sympathetic? Or nothing, to indicate to them our abject poverty? In the end we plumped for beer and cider, which seemed a happy medium. Of course when the valuation officers arrived they seemed so amiable that Anthony and I made one of our usual deplorable errors. We threw caution to the four winds and brought out the whisky and gin; I think we even went so far as to produce the Napoleon brandy. In fact we had an extremely convivial morning. We toured the castle, and our two visitors admired all our improvements with charming old-world courtesy, and praised us on the beauty of the decor. Really it seemed impossible that such delightful people could have anything to do with rates and taxes! Then we all shook hands warmly and they went on their way. Anthony and I congratulated each other on a wonderfully successful day.

How wrong we were! By the time winter had come round again, the blow had fallen. The rates had been put up from £29 to a gross value of £250!

Of course we appealed. Our solicitor told us that we had been rated higher than practically any other house in the county.

Together we worked out facts and figures to prove that the proposed assessment was excessive.

We would explain to the rating appeal board the appalling cost of living with history. We had spent £7,094 on maintenance and £1,502 on improvements. We would also tell them that the place had been saved from becoming a complete ruin, with walls falling down, windows out and floors rotting. Somehow we had to make them understand that even now the place

The King's Room—showing doorway leading to the Newel Stairs
Photo. Eric Davidson

Pixie the pony gate-crashes on a children's party
Photo. Sunday Express

All our pets are making friends. Nimrod, Columbine, Delilah with our two whippets
Clovis and Misty

Photo. Border Press Agency Ltd.

was not waterproof. The windows let in torrents, and the dungeons flooded when it rained. As well as all this, we had to *hod* our own rubbish to the village green.

We were now getting quite excited about the forthcoming battle, but of course on the day that our case was due to come up we were snowed-in. The yews round the church, the fells, the castle battlements and the ludicrous little rusty trees which were meant to be our hedge, were all hidden in a whirling white chaos by daylight. The snow had drifted high over the wheels of the van and it was impossible to dig it out. Fortunately for us, all the members of the local valuation panel were snowed-up too, as was our solicitor, so our case was postponed for a month.

For three days snow flakes as big as the breast feathers of geese fell, and the air was full of the screeching cries of black-backed gulls which had flown inland. The sun tried to shine, but it was a dirty ochre colour without heat or rays, and the heavy drifts of snow became filmed with brittle ice. As it grew colder we began to worry about our birds. We knew that many of the rabbits would be dead in their frozen burrows, and that the foxes would be growing more rapacious. As well as our own birds we now had starlings, crows, finches, wagtails, gulls and robins to feed, but some of the smaller wild birds were becoming too weak to fly and we were conscious that they would soon be eaten by rats, stoats and weasels. One of our peahens was very lame, her claw having been affected by the frost while she was roosting. Every day now we had to take hay on foot to our horses, and buckets of warm water to pour into their troughs in which the water was frozen solid—so solid that we could not even break it with rocks.

We were snowbound for ten days, and our stores were becoming short. I had run out of various tinned commodities due to miscalculation, but we still had a plentiful supply of flour. Every day I baked bread from a simple recipe of self-raising flour, salt and milk, which we could still procure from a nearby farm. It was quite pleasant, but extremely fattening. I have never had any success with dried yeast, not having the mental equipment to spend hours in the kitchen while *this living plant which can be killed by the wrong treatment*, as the cookery books say, sulkily refuses to ferment. There always seems to be something more interesting to do.

I knew that Anthony was getting anxious about his work in London. It was impossible to drive to the station as the road was still under four feet of snow. But the eleventh day of the great freeze-up arrived with mist and drizzle, and the south wind which blew across from Vicarage Hill loosened the ice tentacles from every tree and bush and plant. The thick snowdrifts in our drive melted almost overnight, and Anthony was at last able to get away to London.

But a few hours after I had waved goodbye to him, the thaw also melted the snow from White Stone Moor, which filled the becks that ran into the Eamont, and flooded Ullswater. Even then I was not particularly worried, for I knew that by this time Anthony would be past the flooded road and on his way to London. We still had some stores left, even if the vans could not get through from Penrith. Unfortunately, thanks to my inefficiency, these consisted mainly of porridge and cornflakes, which have since become anathema to us.

Our little beck, which had previously been choked with black ice, was now like a river in spate, as water raced in foaming torrents down the fells.

We were isolated by flooded fields, and even our courtyard was awash. As if there was not already enough water, sheets of rain began to blow across the landscape, altogether hiding the stunted trees on the slopes of the valley. Sky and land merged in a steely expanse of grey.

I was depressed by Anthony's departure because I hated being alone in the castle in the winter. That is, if one could equate being caged up with four children and about a hundred pets with being alone! I think this is why, as I pensively watched the flood waters creeping across the grass and under the door of the dungeons, my reactions were somewhat delayed. The cellar had often been under a couple of inches of water, and it merely meant the rather tedious business of bailing it out with buckets. Then I remembered with an unpleasant shock that the sacks of grain had not yet been poured into their bins, and would probably be afloat by now. Wearily I put on my wellingtons and went down to salvage the debris. Dacre's dungeons are huge and vaulted and consist of two rooms each about 30 feet by 25 feet. Before I had taken one step into them the water was over the top of my boots. The place was awash under 18 inches of dark, filthy water. The grainsacks had rotted and burst. Corn, oats and pony nuts were floating around in a soggy mess. But this was not the worst of it. Floating on top of the slimy surface were 50 or 60 of my oil paintings. These were not perhaps exceptional works of art, but they represented a large chunk of our life. Ever since Anthony and I had started going abroad, I had tried to do one or two paintings of all the fascinating places we had visited. There, drifting among the grain, were sodden little fragments of many happy holidays— paintings of Italy, Spain and Portugal. There under spongy lumps of flaked maize was the portrait of the *Annie Laurie*, a little gaff-rigged ketch which we had sailed from Devonshire to Le Havre and through the French canals to Paris. And there beneath a lump of mud was a portrait of the Alexandre III bridge—the Bridge of the Golden Horses, painted from the left bank where we had been moored. Half hidden by a pile of turkey pellets was our little villa on the Costa del Sol, with its wonderful Cezanne mountain in the background. Unfortunately I had not painted these pictures on canvas, but on daler boards, which are sheets of glorified cardboard with a grained surface. And here they were, literally disintegrating before my eyes! However, I could not stop to salvage my paintings, for I saw that the water had risen to within three inches of the central heating boiler, and that this boiler was at any moment likely to explode.

I dragged a water carrier into the cellar and began to bail frantically. But I soon realized that the task was useless. As soon as I wheeled the water carrier out and tipped the water into the courtyard, it just flooded in again. It was clear that there was nothing for it but to telephone the fire brigade. I began to stumble through the debris to the telephone in the hall. It was inevitable! Our telephone always went wrong in the rain, and this time was no exception. Then I ran to the village, but the phone box there was out of order too and this meant that I must go to Pooley Bridge. The van, of course, was away with Anthony, but even if it had been there, it would have been useless. The road alongside Ullswater was flooded. In desperation I grabbed a bicycle from the garage. At this time of year the hours of daylight were brief and although it was only 4.30 it was already growing dark. The road to Pooley Bridge, which was normally pocked with holes and pits, was now dotted with lakes and pools which ran into each other and swirled over the macadam surface. The peaty water surging along the twin gutters resembled a couple of swollen brooks. I could see the melting snow rushing in foaming rivers down the screes into Ullswater, while the lake was washing over the road in great waves. Ullswater, usually so calm and glossy, looked like an angry sea. A dozen cars were drawn up about a hundred yards from the lake, blocking the road. With my bicycle I managed to make a detour into the soaking wet bracken along the high bank by the side of the road, and my hair was full of twigs and thorn by the time I at last reached Pooley Bridge.

I managed to contact the Carlisle fire brigade from the telephone booth, and they promised to come and help me. Indeed it took me so long to bicycle back up the steep hills that they were at Dacre almost before I was. The floodwater was still rising and was now only an inch from the boiler. The firemen told me that the only way they could successfully pump out the water in time was to take up some flagstones from the floor and dig a hole to put their pump in. Naturally I agreed, and ran to fetch a pick axe.

With their huge pump, two men managed to disperse the water in about ten minutes. It was unbelievable; with my buckets it would have taken days. But what a horrible aftermath! The cellar floor was a terrible mess with its beautiful flagstones broken, and layers of dark filth everywhere. I only managed to salvage three of my paintings. *Annie Laurie* had become a lump of slimy pulp. I was very angry with Anthony when he told me the next day how amused he had been to read on the front pages of the *Evening News* and the *Standard* about

Bunty to the rescue and *The three mile cycle dash for help.*
I still find it rather hard to see the joke!

We were certainly learning about living in castles
the hard way, but we now have a very solid pump
permanently in the dungeon, and no more worries from
that direction.

Three weeks after the flood, the valuation court met in
Penrith Town Hall to enquire into the rates of Dacre
Castle. Miss Mary Reed our solicitor put forward our
case with great lucidity. It was bitterly cold in the court
room, and I noticed three reporters muffled in overcoats
sitting along one of the benches. I imagined them to be
from the local press, and they were taking down the
proceedings in shorthand. Mr. Donald Quarrington,
representing the Cumberland valuation officer, made a
remark that I could not quite understand, as it seemed
to have little bearing on the situation. He said that Mr.
Kinsman was a tenant, not an owner, who had spent
money on the property, and that in modernizing this
twelfth century castle there was prestige value.

After retiring, the chairman said that considering the
restricted market for the type of property, and other
factors, they considered that the suggested assessment
was excessive.

Although we won our case and had £50 taken off
our rates, the whole thing left me with an unpleasant
taste in my mouth. As it turned out the reporters were
not only from the local, but also from the national press,
and all the details of our life in the castle were spread
over the newspapers. Tit bits included how often we
had to cart our dustbins to the village green.

Anthony's sister Anne, who is a barrister, came to
stay a few days before Christmas, and was enchanted
with the district. Indeed it looked wonderful that

December. Ullswater was as still as glass, and the snow that powdered the fells had hardened to splintered patterns of crystal under a brilliant blue sky. As well as Anne, we had another guest for Christmas, Valent an Ibizan greyhound. It was nice to have a dog in the castle again and Valent, which is Spanish for Valiant, was sweet. He was the sort of dog who would sit for hours, his paw on your knee, through hours of boring human talk. His bounding action was very attractive too, reminding me of a fawn. He had been the first of his breed to be brought to Britain from the tiny island near Majorca, and after being put to stud he had become the father of Britain's newest dog family. Unfortunately this had given Valent a propensity to wander, and as Anne lived in an area where there was a lot of heavy traffic she was very tempted to leave him with us. But after our unfortunate experiences with Mustapha and Saki we did not feel that we could accept the responsibility of someone else's dog. I only wish we had kept him, for three months later he was killed after jumping a fence and trotting off to visit a bitch in a nearby village. It seems that in this decade of fast cars, a dog's life has become a thing of extreme vulnerability. We have often been advised by nearby farmers that the only way to keep a dog is tied up on a chain to a ring as they do, or locked in a kennel, and although my mind has sometimes inclined to this point of view, it is a horrifying thought.

A few days after Anne's arrival, Anthony's mother and mine both travelled to stay with us. This was going to be a real family Christmas. They arrived laden with presents, and the castle was immediately turned into a sort of Aladdin's cave. Anthony's mother had brought some Roman glass that his father had dug up in

Damascus. After being buried in the earth for hundreds of years, it had acquired a patina of silver and green. Among the pieces were some tear bottles that the Roman widows used to weep into over their husbands' graves. Because of exposure to the air while being packed and unpacked, some of the glass was beginning to crumble away, but we soon had it installed safely in a cabinet in the King's Room, where it glowed magically.

I loved having our family staying with us, and I knew I was going to miss them terribly when they left. Coming north had made a great crack in our lives and the lives of those who cared for us, and it was five years before I managed to travel up to London; there always seemed to be so many animals and children to look after. I will never forget one day when Anthony and I, bored with domesticity, decided to take off for a whole day on the fells, and Mrs. Wells kindly offered to assume charge of the animals. When we got back, feeling extraordinarily mellow after a day with our horses, we found Mrs. Wells in tears, and the donkey bellowing like a bull with a vastly distended stomach. 'Darling Columbine' had cleverly opened her gate and broken into the dungeons where the stores were kept. Everything was in chaotic disorder with bins of grain spilt, and packets of pony nuts scattered. After this I fear Columbine had drunk her fill at her water tank and was rapidly sinking into a state of coma. Luckily Mrs. Wells, fearing that the donkey's life was in danger, had acted with great presence of mind and telephoned the vet. However, when Mr. B. arrived he merely prodded Columbine once or twice in the stomach remarking laconically: "Aye, it'll take more'n a few sacks o' grain to harm a Jenny. Ye'll find the only thing to ever kill off a donkey is old age!" . . . And he was right! 'Darling Columbine' was quite herself the next day, and from the din that she was making at the gate (to which a strong oak bar had been added) appeared to be quite ready for a repeat performance.

I thought it very gallant of our mothers to come and visit us at all, as they both loathed the country. "All those dripping trees!" complained Anthony's mother. "And all those horrible noises in the night of animals killing each other!" added mine.

Yes, I was going to miss our family, and I knew too that I was going to miss Valent. It would be sad to be without a dog again. When our visitors had left, my spirits became temporarily low, and when I heard of Valent's death something happened to me that has never happened before. I became superstitious. I had the impression that the castle was unlucky. In London I had never been given to fits of depression, but now I became jumpy and nervous, and hated to see the children climbing trees or galloping their ponies. I began to feel that everything and everyone was accident prone. I even began to wonder if the death of our dogs might be some kind of warning. But how ridiculous! Then too, I became superstitious about the peacocks. There are primitive tribes in the East who worship these birds as devils, and in view of subsequent events I think they are right to do so.

A week or two after Christmas, Anthony had to go to London. The lovely, still, frosty weather had been succeeded by fierce winds and heavy downpours. I was sitting alone one evening after the children had gone to bed, listening to the wind's dismal rue, when I heard the back door banging. It must have blown open after an extremely strong gust. The children had just destroyed my last torch and so I lit a candle, but the flame was immediately blown out. To shed some light on the scene I left the door of the Great Hall open, and groped my way down the newel stairs. This was not a particularly pleasant business, as I have already hinted, because the bats were making strange unearthly noises, rather like the rustling of dead leaves being whirled around by the wind. Then I heard a piercing scream. At that moment my scalp began to prickle and my hands waxed clammy.

Fortunately I had left an electric light on in the dungeons in case there was an emergency, and I was soon able to see that it was only Romeo. The strange rustling sound was the agitation of his still diminutive tail before a display, although for whose benefit he was displaying I could not say. He must have been as startled to see me as I was to see him, for he rushed past me with a velocity that nearly knocked me down, and hurtled on up the newel stairs into the Hall.

I panted after him, just in time to see him launch himself upwards to gain a precarious purchase on the ornate gold frame of a valuable painting. He stayed there for a moment or two to crow his diabolical triumph, while the frame which was made of plaster disintegrated between his claws. Then he clattered down to the floor with a terrifying rattle of wings. Relieved that he had not hit the Meissen, I gently drove him towards the newel stairs. I knew that it would be useless to entice him down toward the garden as birds hate flying downwards, so I drove him upwards to the battlements, and it was a wonderful sight the next morning to see him soaring down to the ash tree from the top of a crenellated tower.

But back to that painting. It was a Plether, of which

Anthony was extremely fond, and although I did not care for it much, I thought he would be rather upset to see the destruction of the frame. The painting was about four feet by three feet and hung at least seventeen feet above the ground, so I went in search of a long ladder, and later that night I restored the frame with plastic wood, gilded it, and the next morning prepared to rehang the finished effort on the wall. With the exertion of reaching up, and with the weight of the frame, I overbalanced and the ladder slipped from underneath me. The Plether caught on the corner of a cupboard and the canvas was split from end to end. Of course it had been a stupid thing for me to attempt to do, but I could not help blaming the peacock, and I maintain that there is something in the superstition that peacocks are unlucky. There is still a large dent in the floor where I fell. It may have been caused by the ladder, but I rather suspect it was my head!

Of course when Anthony saw the state of his favourite picture, he thought I had done it on purpose. After all, I had never liked the thing!

8 Ghosts from the Past

"Is the castle haunted?"

I think I must have been asked this question hundreds of times during our first summer. Generally I laughed and replied that it would be a rare ghost which could survive electric light and central heating. It is well-known that both these things are death to ghosts. And indeed at that time I did not seriously think that there was anything spooky about the castle. Sombre it might look from the outside, and possibly unwelcoming; once inside, however, the impression was of the deepest peace and domesticity.

But nature is in itself magical and mysterious, and I found that after two years of living among the mountains I was acquiring, without realising it, some of the troubling supernatural beliefs of the Lake District. Although I still scoffed at people—including the wife of a farmer, a veracious old soul, who had once lived here —when I was told that there was a ghost in the castle, I was beginning to wonder if it were possible for other forms of life to exist on different vibrations, and if there were more things in heaven and earth . . .

About this time I began to look into the castle's history more diligently. I spent many happy hours in Penrith Library, and I own to becoming extremely absorbed in the curious tales from Dacre's past. Whenever possible though, I would borrow the books and read them at home, for there was something about our home, with its mediaeval atmosphere, that lent itself to all that whispered of the unearthly and the strange. The age of the building alone, made the transition from one period to another extraordinarily easy.

I sifted the stories and found that some were mere *fabulae* and *winter's tales*. But two of them were factual enough. My first interesting find was the reproduction of a portrait of Mary Neville, Baroness Dacre. She was sitting stiffly in a high-backed chair, her huge body sustained almost rigid by the stiffness of her black gown. Her plump face was as bland as a baby's, but she had a childish pout, and strange eyebrows drawn in a thin, hard line. Beneath the portrait was a short note which mentioned that the husband of the Baroness had been hanged for murder. A short time afterwards I was lucky enough to find an old engraving, copied from a portrait of the Baron. The infinitely pure lines of his thin, mediaeval face stood out from a black ground as if they had been carved from marble. It was a face with no softness about it, but it had considerable charm.

"Poor Lady Dacre", I thought. "Fat, ageing and unattractive; obviously her handsome young husband murdered her!" But here my sense of history was deficient. I had forgotten that the men of those days liked their women fat . . . In Penrith archives I discovered that the Baron had been executed for the murder of his gardener. How absurd to be lucky enough to have a gardener and then to murder him!

The last male heir of the house of Dacre, the most formidable of the Cumberland families, met with a tragic fate. When only a year old the little boy was thrown from a wooden jousting horse. He had two sisters. Philip, Earl of Arundel divided the vast Dacre estates by marrying one of the heiresses, while his brother Lord William Howard secured the other. This struck me as being a pathetic story, and not without its sinister implications.

It was on the first of January, 1967, that one of our summer visitors sent me the Legend of Dacre Castle. It consists of five pages, closely written, and photostated from an old manuscript, and it is a story which, ever since I read it, has stuck unpleasantly in my mind like a burr.

Heading these dry pages is an engraving of a miniature of the Lady Eloise, daughter of the famous Constable St. Pol. She was a beauty of the late Renaissance. The face is ivory-skinned and oval. The forehead is high and round. The lids, over large cold eyes, are heavy and a little drawn at the corners. The tight, thin lips, so opposed to the out-turned flesh of today's mouths, give to the face a strange air of aristocracy and mystery, plus a sinister seductiveness.

The legend states that at the age of 20, Guy Langdale, son and heir of Lord Dacre, was placed under the tuition of the Constable and old friend of his father. Here he completed his education, learnt the art of fencing, and also fell violently in love with his host's daughter, the beautiful Lady Eloise. But it appears that the young girl, who was at this time pursued by a veritable army of suitors, took little interest in the Englishman.

Guy had a bosom friend, "a handsome young man, blonde and olive-skinned", called Montalet des Roches. He was guitar master and Italian instructor to Eloise, and it was to Montalet that he went for help. Somewhat flippantly, the unscrupulous young tutor agreed to help the affair forward.

It is easy to imagine the Lady Eloise sitting in her private garden and watching Guy Langdale through half-closed eyelids. He was a big, handsome man with a fair complexion; the sort of Christian soldier who would stand stiff as a tapestry warrior. But his courting technique did not match his masterly appearance. He was shy, bashful and not at all a sweeper-of-women-off-their-feet. Eloise was far from impressed, and, when he proposed marriage, turned him down flat. He, in turn, was hurt, embarrassed and somewhat jealous. For Eloise made it clear that, in spite of his wealth, he was not the only fish in the sea. Thus goaded, he swore to kill any rival for her hand. Eloise was smugly content. It looked like being a good fight!

As it happened, Guy had other battles on his hands. He was summoned back to England to fight the Scots who were ravaging the Border Country. For three years the skirmishing went on, and the young Lord Dacre performed yeoman service amongst the mists of the Cumbrian hills.

When he eventually revisited the Continent, the Constable St. Pol welcomed him as an eligible son-in-law, and the Lady Eloise, apparently much mellowed, accompanied him submissively to the altar. Montalet des Roches was groomsman, and after the cremony he accompanied the happy couple to Dacre Castle on the shores of Ullswater.

I have found an entry in my diary for January 3rd 1967. Apparently it was about this time that I put the manuscript away, having decided not to continue reading it. I think I felt already that there would be something unpleasant about its conclusion—although no doubt anything morbid in it could be put down to the usual mythopoeic tendencies of the Renaissance.

For a few days I was busy marking and preparing the children's school clothes, but after the term had started I began to feel prey to a peculiar restlessness. Anthony was working in London and the castle seemed silent and lonely. The land was once again covered with snow as far as the eye could see. It shrouded the leafless trees and the rough grass and reeds. The sky was low and heavy with the cruel cold. The castle alone looked dark against all this whiteness.

I wandered restlessly through the vast rooms watching the grey day dwindle into the ghostly silence of dusk, and tried to find jobs to do that would hold my attention. I remember making a rather weighty chocolate cake for the children, and then took up one book after another and discarded them. I even tried to learn a few tunes on Amanda's guitar, but it was all to no avail, for what I really wanted to do was to read the manuscript. And after all, was it not ridiculous to be nervous about something which had happened at least 400 years previously?

I did not begin to read until 10 o'clock, by which time the wind had risen, blowing the snow in drifts round the courtyard and moaning softly through the battlements. But soon I was so engrossed that I did not even hear it.

Weeks rolled by; months passed. The Lord of Dacre became the proud father of a fine boy. Friend Montalet stood Godfather.

But now the Scots were on the war-path once more, and Lord Guy was required by King Henry to organize the defence. Before riding out from Dacre, he constituted Montalet des Roches his castellan and guardian of his wife and child. He also placed his small garrison under the command of a faithful seneschal Lyulph.

And so two years wore on. Life at the castle was dull. Heather, sheep, rain and mist are unexciting companions. When the Court visited York, the Count des Roches lost no time in taking Lady Dacre along to savour the gaiety and

Sapphia practises bull-fighting with Edward the Swaledale
Photo. Robert Armstrong

Jezebel, our one-year-old Indian kestrel, ready for dinner
Photo. Daily Mail

Bedroom—formerly a chapel

Photo. Eric Davidson

grandeur of it all. And, as was to be expected, their visit occasioned no small amount of tongue-wagging and head-shaking.

The Lord of Dacre was encamped at Brampton when news of his wife's scandalous behaviour reached him. Although slightly wounded, he rode to York and made straight for the inn where she was lodged. From behind the arras in her bedroom he had confirmation of her liaison with his friend and confidant Montalet. His fury was great, but he kept his peace and sent a servant after Montalet, who left soon afterwards for Dacre.

The hunt was on!

I had been poring over the manuscript for nearly an hour, when I became disturbed by a sudden stillness. Outside the wind had risen and was now raging down the valley, but inside there was no sound except the whisper of the wind's rue through the turrets, and now and then the hiss of sleet as it splashed down the big open chimney during a lull in the storm. The fire of cedar logs had fallen low and the embers were growing pale. The figures in the tapestries glimmered dimly in the fading red glow, evoking an aura of forgotten days. Suddenly I shivered. The castle seemed eery that night. It was too full of impressions of the past. But I could not leave the legend unfinished, and although it was late I built up the fire and continued reading.

With Montalet out of the way, Lord Guy lost no time in confronting Eloise with her infidelity. At first she tried to brazen it out. Then, sensing that all was lost, she threw discretion to the wind, admitted the affair, and made it clear that she had obtained a great deal of pleasure from it.

Lord Guy's fury was cold and calculating. Without delay he had his wife sent back to Dacre. When she arrived there, she was escorted to her personal chamber, and the door was locked on her. Seated in a corner was her lover. She ran to him. Her arms embraced him. Her lips sought his.

But there was no response. With horror she realised that Montalet was dead, murdered at her husband's command. The corpse had been bequeathed to her! And for ten years, in that tiny chamber, it was her silent and solitary companion. Embalmed and ageless, it crouched by her, while she wrinkled and drooped to senility. Lord Guy and she never met again . . .

After I had finished reading I sat gazing into the dying embers for a long time. The past was so imprinted on my mind that I could not summon the courage to go to my bedroom. It seems to me ridiculous now but I felt that this was the room where Eloise had found her tutor. I could imagine so vividly those years when the beautiful woman lived shut up with that corpse. My fingers itched to claw at the few rotten shreds of clothing. I am an agnostic, but in spite of this I have often longed to find some evidence of a being or thing which could make me believe in an after-life. But of course I have never been successful.

Nevertheless for weeks afterwards I was still so absorbed in the legend that I spent most of my free time in the archives of the local libraries. On the 31st of January I made another entry in my diary. I had found a second engraving. It was of Lady Eloise of Dacre without any doubt. Here were the same narrow hands, the long slender neck, the bared forehead and the same air of disdainful haughtiness. It was a cruel face, except that beauty is never cruel, only indifferent. Perhaps this was the tragedy of Eloise St. Pol. But this leaves one in the air, as in those unsatisfactory short stories by modern writers. On the 3rd of February, according to an entry in my diary, my story had even less form, and I was left even more confused, for as well as having no heroine, I now had no hero!

After Christmas we found ourselves very short of grazing for Columbine and Edward, as our small field had become a mud patch. The vicar agreed to rent the churchyard to us as long as we put up an electric fence to keep the animals from the graves. I was a little worried about this as there were a lot of yews planted round St. Andrews. These are dangerous to animals, but only if the branches are broken or dying, so we kept a sharp eye on them. After filling the animals' trough with water I often used to visit the church to study the architecture, which was reputed to be Norman. It was on my third visit that I discovered the effigy dressed in armour, man-size in stone. At the base among some crumbling scrolls, reversed and interwoven, I discovered the initials *G.L.* The sandstone face of the sleeping warrior was somewhat worn away, giving it an expression that was both hard and cruel.

9 *Feathers and All That*

I REALISED by this time that I had been steeping myself too much in history, and becoming too absorbed in the visionary old-world atmosphere of my castle. I think I was even imagining that there might be some sinister connection between our own misfortunes and the events of the past!

This is why I was so delighted when Anthony brought a box from the station on the morning of my birthday. When I opened it, there was whippet puppy scarcely bigger than my hand. He was fawn with a grey mask and dark, rather surprised eyebrows. It was wonderful to have a puppy in the house again. We fed him on mince-meat, puppy meal and milk, four times a day, and called him Crusoe, after one of the hounds from the local hunt. This huge foxhound had been a constant visitor to the castle ever since our first hunt meeting there.

Ullswater Hunt is not a Christmas card affair of brilliant pink coats and high stepping horses, but a Lakeland equivalent. Because of the rugged nature of the land the men of the Lakes hunt on foot—those, that is, who do not merely follow in cars. They are clad in cloth caps, tweeds and hob-nailed boots that are laced right up the ankle. They arm themselves with stout shepherds' crooks to help them up the precipitous screes, and carry macks against the icy rain that usually drenches the fells throughout the winter months.

When we heard that the hunt met once a year at Dacre, on the village green, we suggested to the master that he should have an annual meet at the castle and start the morning off with a *cup*. Fortunately we had inherited an old punch bowl, and Mrs. Wells and I made the punch which consisted of rum, hot water, lemon, nutmeg and cinnamon. We also had ginger beer for the children from the village.

Our one worry was how our peafowl would react to the hounds, and in view of what happened next our fears were well-founded. As soon as the hounds were let through our gate they tore into the open-fronted garage where the peafowl were roosting, and put them up. The two hens and the two cocks soared up to the battlements where they perched in a row, glaring balefully at the hounds until the pack was eventually taken off and uncoupled at Salmond's Wood. Joe Wear admitted to me afterwards that in all his 46 years as huntsman, his hounds had never roused anything quite so unusual.

After a negative season owing to the Arctic conditions, this particular day ended with the capture of three foxes. Personally we were relieved, for after the loss of our Mandarins and Carolinas we had stocked up with some domestic ducks which we were anxious not to lose in the same way. We had been given some black East Indian ducks by a gamekeeper friend; their plumage turns to shining blue and green in the winter. We had also bought two Shelducks with attractive markings of tan, black, and white, a pair of pretty White Call ducks, and a pair of Pochards or diving ducks. After our first disasters, thanks to the hunt, we were not particularly worried by foxes, but we once saw a black cat, almost as big as a panther, which had been abandoned and gone wild, jump the sheep wire fence with one of the black ducks in its mouth. The pond eventually proved too muddy for the Pochards with their diving habits, and sadly, after two years, they died. After three years the Shelducks wandered away, but now, at the end of five years, we still have the black ducks and eleven sooty little ducklings together with the White Call ducks. Of course, like most of our animals and birds, they have become too tame, and spend most of their time squatting in the courtyard, or more usually under the van, instead of looking picturesque on the pond.

After we had held one or two meets at Dacre Castle we found that the foxhounds often used to turn up there in the evening if they had been hunting anywhere in the district. I think over the months we have had visits from Ranter, Railer, Bellman, and possible True—not forgetting Crusoe.

Crusoe's visits were definitely a mixed blessing, for when he found out that he could possibly get a meal of biscuits at the castle he became rather crafty. On some days he would completely ignore the huntsman's van and make his way straight to Dacre. Although a charming dog, his manners were oafish in the extreme. I think in his kennels he must have been fairly high up in the order of the bench, for no sooner would he nose through the front door, than our own dogs would find themselves roughly pushed off the bench—a comfortable red sofa, in this case—and on to the floor.

Of course as soon as we rang the kennels, Maldwyn Williams, the young Welsh whipper-in, with his usual conscientious efficiency, would be round to collect the truant. I was extremely impressed by the way he identified one hound from another, for they used to all look much the same to me. When I hopefully said to him "Is that Ruby?" he would ponder for a moment counting the notches in one floppy ear and then say "No, not Ruby. That's Ruby's daughter, Remedy!"

Amanda's birthday was soon after mine. As she was at school and had not much time to care for a puppy, we answered an advertisement in *Exchange and Mart* for a black whippet of 18 months called Ringo.

The station master at Penrith is something of a wit and he rang me up on Amanda's birthday to say that he had good news for us. Hi Jo was waiting to be collected at the station. (Hi Jo was a valuable black greyhound which had recently been kidnapped.) The station master's joke was rather too near the truth for comfort. This dog certainly looked more like a greyhound than a whippet. He was big and rangy like a long dog in a Georgian sporting print. He was also extremely thin, with all the fur worn from his tail. This made it look like one of those sad ox-tails you see in butchers' shops. But he was extremely gentle, and Amanda took to him immediately. She renamed him Clovis. I think his master had been kind, for Clovis was wearing a somewhat worn coat and a nice collar; but apparently the young man had been having domestic difficulties and his dogs had had to sleep in a shed. The next day we took Clovis to the vet to see what could be done about his worn fur. The vet told us that this had probably been caused by sleeping on hard boards. Now Clovis never sleeps anywhere but on Amanda's bed, and his coat has been in perfect condition ever since. In fact he is curled upon the eiderdown now as I write. Clovis' rakish appearance is heightened by a torn ear, which his master says is due to a tangle with a fox. This I can well believe, for he is ready to take on any dog in a fight, whatever the size. Odds mean nothing to him!

In the new year we rode out on the fells whenever we could. I found that by wearing warm tights under my jodhpurs, with my chin tucked well into the collar of my anorak, I could keep warm enough. There is something exhilarating about being out when the gales are sweeping down the valley and over the hills. Everything appears to be in motion, the wind-blown firs, the decayed bracken, the rowans by the becks almost bending double but never seeming to break. Although at this time of year the fells are bare and the landscape barren, there is such movement in the sky that the scenery is even more beautiful than it is in summer.

Nimrod was growing up, and now that he was weaned I had begun to ride Sheba again. Of course her son refused to be left behind and would follow his mother across five or six miles of fells like an extremely well-behaved dog, jumping logs and streams when she did. When Crusoe was six months old we felt that we could begin to exercise him on the fells too. There were a great many hares that winter. On fine days they would be sitting up on their hind legs, ears pricked forward, but on cold days we would see them lying in their grass hollows, with brown fur fluffed out and ears pinned back. I must admit that on those days when we saw a great number of hares, we often used to have the most delicious roast saddle tied up in bacon for lunch, whilst the remains would make the dogs an excellent dinner. As well as these intriguing hares, Crusoe had a cache of interesting toys on the fells. Old sheep's heads that he would use as rattles, before hiding them in the bracken; bleached bones that lay scattered over the grass, and his favourite, a bright silver tin can which he would roll down the screes, trying to catch it with his paws and bite it. It was a curious thing but he never once forgot where he had hidden his toys. He could find them again at any given moment.

By mid-May when the buds of the fallen ash by our pond at last began to open hopefully, we had begun to forget the sad events of the previous winter. The deaths of Mustapha and Saki were already sinking into the pattern that was the past.

In June, Juliet went missing. It was Ivan who eventually found her in a scooped-out hollow in a patch of nettles by my rose bed. In the Autumn Anthony had hacked out this bed through the inevitable solid stone, and I had planted some sturdy little bushes in it: Nevadas, Albertines, Sweet Briars and Queen Elizabeths. They were all flourishing and the only eyesore on the horizon was the nettle patch that I had intended to remove before the season started. Now it was impossible. It would be weeks before I could get out the scythe, because a peahen sits for a full 28 days.

We became rather worried about Juliet towards the end, as she was becoming very thin. She seldom left her nest and we dared not leave food too near her in case it attracted predators. She would occasionally soar over the fence honking loudly for food. When this happened, Anthony or I would immediately drop whatever we were doing to rush out with turkey-rearing pellets and chopped hard-boiled egg. But on these occasions she always seemed distrait and rather hysterical. She would take only one or two pecks at the food and water before flying back to her five eggs. Miss Evans told me to scatter the eggs with water whenever I got the chance, but this was usually a race against time as Juliet did not like me going near them. I think she was really too young and flighty to be a mother, for after three and a half weeks she lost patience and began to peck at her eggs, and one day we found her attacking a shell so vigorously that she actually cracked it open. Inside was an embryo chick almost ready to hatch. Before the 28 days were up, Juliet had cracked open and stamped on three more of her eggs. We found their blooded remains around the one perfect egg that was left.

But on the 28th day—success at last! Juliet came strutting on to the front lawn with one tiny brown and yellow chick in tow. This pea chick became for us an interesting, though sad, study in psychology. She was a nice little hen, very gentle and friendly, and devoted to her mother. But when in the following Spring Juliet reared another family, successfully hatching out five chicks this time, she abandoned her eldest daughter and by so doing completely ruined her character. Drucilla, as we subsequently called her, turned into one of the most diabolical birds I have ever known. She became jealous and spiteful. Alone among our pea fowl she is a real danger to the bantam chicks, and in the last year she has accounted for at least five of them.

In the July of 1967 my sister Sonia and my brother-in-law Julien Melchett paid us a fleeting visit. Julien had once been a pilot in the Fleet Air Arm and now he always flew his own plane. The journey from Norfolk to Carlisle had only taken about an hour, and my sister arrived in a white linen coat, looking as pretty and uncreased as if she had just stepped out of a page in *Vogue*. This was a wonderful surprise visit and she arrived laden with flowers from her garden in Norfolk. Surreptitiously, while Anthony was mixing the martinis, I slipped away and changed from my grubby jodhpurs, into something more respectable. Thank heavens, I thought, there was a chicken in the fridge!

It was a glorious day, and I was delighted because Romeo, who was now in all his feathered finery, had decided to roost high up in the ash tree outside the window of the big hall where we were having lunch. There, framed in the window, was a true Indian tapestry, the proud magnificent bird with his long tail feathers floating down among the leaves, each eye of immortality shining with deep blues and phosphorescent greens, the tips sprinkled with gold or bronze according to how they caught the light.

The ash tree was Romeo's favourite roosting place in fine weather, for he seldom roosted with his wives, particularly if they were broody.

We began lunch with *chicken maringo*. I had fortunately got some grapes and had managed to whip up one of those hot and cold sweets *grapes à la neige*. This is one of our favourites as it is not too stodgy. The grapes are pipped and chilled, then covered with whipped cream and a thick coating of demerara sugar. This is quickly turned to fudge under the grill.

We were just starting on the Gruyère when I noticed with an uneasy sense of foreboding that Romeo had left his perch in the ash tree and had flown to join Juliet on an uncomfortable square beam in front of the garage. This is something he only does in summer if there is a storm approaching. I did not know if I was still superstitious about the peacocks, but one thing I have never doubted is their reliability as barometers.

Sonia and Julien had intended to stay until the evening, but they had had a fairly bumpy flight over the Pennines in their single-engined plane, on their way to Dacre, and they did not want to repeat the performance in a storm. Although the sky was a brilliant blue as we waved goodbye after lunch, sure enough the storm started over the east fells only a couple of hours later. Thank goodness my sister and her husband were well on their way past the danger zone by that time, and already over Norfolk.

It was only a few days after Romeo had given us this timely warning, that tragedy struck. I had been watching him on the lawn. He looked proud and fantastically beautiful as he displayed his outspread tail to his harem of hens. I went to scatter some turkey-rearing pellets for him about the grass, and he picked them up with a delicacy and deliberation which was enchanting to watch. When he had finished eating he departed for the village—I imagined, to review the lettuce situation.

When I went into the garden about an hour later I saw him gaining an unsteady purchase on the gate before tumbling on to the lawn. When I went over to him I found that he was dead. His neck was limp and his dark, basilisk eyes, already filmed with grey. We could only assume that in the village he must have eaten some slug pellets, which are so similar to turkey-rearing pellets, and poisoned himself.

We now had to fall back on the *Exchange and Mart* peacock, our second string. I had recently named him Nureyev because of the elegant and somewhat ritualistic dances he performed in the paddock on a block of cement which had once been the foundation of a little cottage. These dances, accompanied by plaintive screeches to the disinterested hens, had somehow reminded me, with their peculiar delicacy and elegance, of a ballet dancer eternally practising on an empty stage in a theatre with no audience. But now was the time for curtain call. Romeo's lawn was now his, as were the peahens, the garage and the big ash tree. Before long Nureyev was as responsible a father and leader of the peafowl as Romeo had ever been!

10 Bats Hate Falcons

Sᴏᴍᴇ of the least attractive aspects of our new life were the bats, the mice, the wood lice and the various creepy-crawlies which were forever trying to invade the castle. The bats were now back in their hundreds. Crowds of them would hang upside down from the boards above the windows of the newel stairs. Every time I had to go down to the cellars, which was usually about twice a day to empty the kitchen rubbish, or to fetch grain for the birds, my skin would undulate in terror. I think it was inconsistent of me to be so fond of our birds, our animals and our hamsters, and to so dislike the bats. Was this because they were not particularly pretty? They appeared very harmless, although messy, and when I looked at them closely, they seemed to me to have rather sweet little sad faces. But I could not suppress a feeling of utter horror and disgust when, on the badly-lit staircase, they swooped anywhere near my face or hair.

Anthony remembered how falcons had been used to drive away flocks of gulls and pigeons from aerodrome runways during the war, and he wondered if they might have the same effect on our bats. I looked up a book on falconry written by a friend of ours, Humphrey Ap Evans, and discovered that kestrels had once been used for flying after bats in France. I did not think it would be particularly practical to fly the falcons at our bats as they would probably break all our new lattice windows, but I had an idea that their very presence might act as a deterrent. They might also scare the mice which were becoming a perfect pest, nesting among our clothes, nibbling their way into the linen cupboard, and making great holes in the contents.

We had heard that it was difficult to get a licence for English falcons, so Anthony contacted an import firm and had two female kestrels flown from India. The reason we chose females was that they are slightly bigger than males.

In ancient times there was a rather class-conscious snobbish formula for falconry:

An eagle for an emperor
A gyrfalcon for a king
A peregrine for an earl
A saker for a knight
A lanner or lagger for a squire
A merlin for a lady
And a kestrel for a knave.

Although during our five years at the castle we have had a saker, a lagger and a merlin, we thought it advisable to start our apprenticeship with kestrels. I now think that this old-fashioned jingle was extremely insulting to these delightful little birds, for they are true falcons with long wings and beautiful dark eyes. They fly high and hover in the same manner as peregrines. They are not carrion eaters.

While we were impatiently waiting for the birds to be flown over from India we read as many books on falconry as we could lay our hands on, to gain as much knowledge as we could of this difficult subject.

It was three weeks before the kestrels reached London, but during this time we were kept fairly busy.

Anthony constructed two perches from Humphrey's instructions which were extremely lucid. He covered a broom handle with deck-chair canvas, and added a lead-weighted screen of the same material, which hung below the perch to enable the birds to regain their balance should they *bait*. I was responsible for the jesses which I cut out from calf skin—and how I hoped that they would fit. For days I had been practising tying them around a pencil. I was also responsible for the little hoods, which act as the equivalent of blinkers, to calm the birds, and I think here my course in millinery and my experience over making Ascot hats must have helped, because they were very pretty, with little peacock feathers for decoration.

At last the great day arrived. The kindly station master at Penrith telephoned us:

"Mr. Kinsman, there's some livestock for you here. Going quite mad, I can tell you—bumping and fluttering in their boxes."

"Thank you," Anthony shouted down the telephone, "I'll be right over for them." Then remembering how these Indian kestrels would probably hate our little chilly wind-blown station: "In the meantime please could you put the boxes somewhere warm?"

Unfortunately Anthony had to leave for London that evening and so we had not time to attach the birds to their perches. Instead Anthony transferred them from their small cardboard boxes into the tin-lined, damp-proof old trunk where Edward had lived as a young lamb. He closed the lid. The latch was broken, so we weighted it with a couple of wooden bars, and drilled holes in the sides for air.

The following morning I had one of my inevitable disasters, one of those disasters which always seem to occur when Anthony is away. I carefully warmed some chunks of beef in my hand to get them to blood heat, with the intention of slipping them into the trunk. I was just squeezing a tempting chunk through one of the holes we had drilled when all nine peafowl swept through the outhouse door which I had stupidly left ajar. They swooped in a body on to the wooden beam above the trunk, and the falcons immediately burst out. I bolted, slamming the door behind me, and left the birds to sort out their differences. Would the falcons eat the peafowl or vice versa? I was not quite sure. As it turned out, when Anthony got back and marched in to survey the holocaust, all the birds seemed to be on amicable terms. But Anthony was not pleased! Now I think that perhaps once more we had beginners' luck for I have since heard of a strange occurrence in a nearby wildlife park.

One evening two vultures were perching picturesquely on a dead branch where they were joined by five or six peafowl. In the morning the vultures had disappeared. On closer inspection the keeper found their dead bodies in the long grass, beneath their perch. The peacocks had killed them.

At dusk Anthony managed to recapture the kestrels from a ladder, for they had perched on one of the highest beams. He returned them to their trunk. We then drove out the furious peafowl and lit a paraffin stove to warm the birds.

An hour later, after a stiff martini, we were back in the mews, which was our new name for the outhouse. By dim candle-light we inspected the hawking furniture, to make sure it was all there. Four jesses, two leashes made from porpoise hide begged from our saddler, two left-handed gauntlets, and two lazy swivels from a fishing tackle shop. In the corner the paraffin stove glowed cosily.

Gingerly Anthony raised the lid of the trunk and I caught a glimpse of a piercing eye. Slowly and quietly he put in a hand and slid it over one of the bird's wings. Then he lifted her out. In the flickering candle-light I saw her close-to for the first time.

The sienna breast feathers were streaked down with dark amber. The claws were a rather pale yellow. They should have been a nice deep gold, but this was probably due to some deficiency in her diet during the journey. The remedy was apparently to dip her raw meat into yolk of egg. On either side of the beak were indistinct moustachial stripes. And the eyes—well it is hard to describe them! Even in these small birds of prey they were quite beautiful, large and lustrous, brownish-black and at this moment burning with a frightened yet revengeful light. We decided on the spot to call the bird Jezebel. While I attempted to fasten the little bird's jesses, her long tallons clutched out nervously at my hands. It all seemed very different from working on a pencil! As I was getting nowhere, Anthony covered up the angry little head with his handkerchief. This had the effect of calming her. After once more frantically studying the diagrams in my books on falconry, I got both jesses, the swivel and the leash safely on. Then I tied the leash to the perch with a special hawking knot, which I had previously mastered. Fortunately these knots came fairly easily to us after a course that we had taken in sailing and navigation before taking our yacht to Paris; they differed very little from the knots used in seafaring. The second little kestrel was very like Jezebel, but she had a more snaky head, and was a good deal thinner. It also struck me that she had a slightly foolish expression. We named her Nefertiti. When we were satisfied that the falcons were comfortable, we left them staring balefully at each other from their respective perches and thankfully retired to bed.

We had decided not to begin *manning* our falcons until the following day. The journey had unnerved them and they needed rest. Nevertheless, for us there was no rest. At half-hourly periods throughout the night we would wake from a haunted sleep, with nightmare images of our kestrels baiting from their perches and hanging from their jesses. Our fears were groundless. In the morning we found them sitting contentedly on their perches with their streaked feathers smooth and trim, while they stared at us with enigmatic eyes.

Behind drawn curtains, with the aid of a single candle and endless glasses of whisky, Anthony and I began the long process of watching and waking. For two days and two nights we watched the sleepless birds until they eventually accepted their strange new perches—our falconer's gloves, and deigned to sleep. In this way, and this way only, could we gain their confidence.

By the following day Jezebel and Nefertiti were even eating, somewhat pettishly, from the fist. By the end of one week they had avidly consumed ounces of tender beefsteak, three lots of pigeon, and a saddle of hare, and were throwing up their pellets of fur and feather with praiseworthy regularity.

We were not going to train our kestrels to fly at any kind of quarry, for there is little that they can catch besides mice and voles, but we concentrated on our primary objective, to rid the castle of bats. Every night we fed the birds in the hall, a rather messy business, with fur and feathers generally scattered all over the Persian rugs, and then carried them down the newel stairs to their mews. After a week the bats were definitely growing more elusive, and after a month I hardly ever saw one at all. Unfortunately the mice were not so sensitive to the kestrels' presence, and we had to resort to traps again.

Feeding our falcons was an extremely time-consuming business, so when the weather was fine we fed them outside on block perches which we had constructed out of the bases of some old stone statues. I had some very embarrassing moments, while showing the public round the castle, for sometimes the visitors would be appalled to see the falcons tucking into a large juicy mouse or rat. However well I hid these banquets in the long grass they always seemed to be very much in evidence. In the end I gave the birds beefsteak on Open Days, and it is extraordinary how the visitors' scruples diminished as the size of the animal eaten increased.

One of our chief anxieties in *manning* the falcons was how they would react to the children. For this reason, during the first few weeks we fed them at night after the children had gone to bed. Our children are rather too well endowed with natural effervescence, and we had an idea that their shouting and yelling might frighten the birds and possibly give them a fit. But oddly enough after Jezebel and Nefertiti had been gradually introduced to the children, they seemed to take to one another. It was rather a sweet sight to see Sebastian and Ivan, aged three and four respectively, sitting sedately for hours watching television with two proud wild birds on their fists, while the falcons themselves stood comfortably on one leg, or roused themselves, contentedly fluffing out their feathers. Sometimes they even dozed with their heads tucked into their wings.

The reactions of Clovis and Crusoe to the falcons was curious. Until the birds had arrived on the scene they had never evinced the slightest trace of jealousy. Now uncomprehendingly they watched us, their masters and sole companions, wasting hours on what they considered to be useless and somewhat abhorrent creatures. Eventually Crusoe began to tolerate the birds, although he never slept in their presence. He only lay on the sofa watching them with a puzzled and hurt expression. Clovis on the other hand would not even sit down with us when the falcons were in the castle. As soon as Jezebel and Nefertiti were brought in from their mews he would stalk out of the room and sulk on one of the children's beds until the coast was clear again.

We were worried about the moulting season. This is normally an extremely difficult period for falcons, and it is often advisable to set the birds free before they begin to moult. But owing to the bat situation we decided to risk the kestrels moulting in captivity and merely let them loose in their mews. Fortunately Jezebel and Nefertiti both survived the trauma successfully.

When Humphrey Ap Evans and his wife Cherry came to see us from Scotland, we were relieved to hear that they thought the birds were looking fit, and that the arrangements for their mews were ideal.

Nefertiti as usual fluttered about in her rather foolish way, but Jezebel sat on her perch as static as an obelisk, allowing herself to be stroked with the goose quill which we kept specially for the purpose. She really was the most tactful bird possible.

Our first assessment of the characters of our two falcons was correct. Nefertiti was always rather a flighty bird. Possibly she was a little old when we

imported her. There is a phrase from Shakespeare's
Othello which explains the situation rather beautifully:
If I do prove her haggard
Though that her jesses were my dear heart-strings
I'd whistle her off, and let her down the wind
To prey at fortune.

Well, I was not expecially attached to Nefertiti, but
she had definitely proved haggard, and so we decided
to hack her back to the open country before the weather
became too cold, and while the north to south migration
of the wild kestrels and merlins was in full swing.
Although something of a flipperty-gibbet, Nefertiti
never particularly wanted to leave us, and setting her
free was not as easy as it sounds.

Once in a fit of pique over some reprimand, one of the
children had surreptitiously untied her leash and let her
go. But she had merely flown to join the pigeons in
the garage—not to kill them, I might say, but merely
to perch beside them in a companionable manner. As
her leash was conveniently hanging down, it was an
easy matter to recapture her. This was a great relief,
for as she still had her jesses on together with her leash,
she could easily have hung herself up on a tree.

Now we removed the jesses and let her fly free. She
swooped once or twice around the battlements and
then we saw her soaring over the big oaks in the
paddock straight into the sunset. Next morning she
was back again, perching on the balustrade outside the
front door. We threw her some steak, and continued
feeding her every day that week. However we did not
want her to be completely dependent on us and so we
began to subsidise her on only two or three days a week.
After a time she flew off to the Divisions, where there
was evidently good hunting, and we saw less of her.

But every now and then we still spot a kestrel hovering over the new plantation and wonder if it is Nefertiti. I hope so. A lot of kestrels around here are trapped in sparrow traps, and I would hate her to be one of them.

Our kestrels had often appeared on television, but now Jezebel was our sole star. This was probably just as well, as Nefertiti usually ruined the films anyway.

I will never forget one nightmarish interview when a very smooth young man arrived from one of our regional studios and invited me to tell him all about falconry. The talk was to take three minutes at the most, and it was to be "precise but brief". The young man thought it would be an amusing idea if he held a falcon himself, and Anthony arranged Jezebel carefully on his hand, winding the leash in the correct way round his fingers. With a sinking heart I realised that I had drawn Nefertiti.

The young man told me not to be nervous. Then as the sound track was switched on I launched into my carefully prepared summary on falconry. But the excitement of seeing strangers proved too much for Nefertiti. As soon as the cameras started to whirl, she bated wildly from my fist and hung upside-down. I pretended not to notice and flicked her back on to my wrist, trying to smile, but silently raging. During those ghastly three minutes the flurry was almost continuous. Amanda had been told to trot into the garden on her pony while I was talking, but of course when Leprechaun saw Nefertiti beating her wings he reared, and Amanda nearly fell off. Then pandemonium broke loose. Ivan chose this moment to tear into the garden with chocolate all over his face, and fell down flat on his face in front of the cameras. He then commenced to yell his head off. Columbine, thinking that something was wrong with one of her darlings, started to roar from her field. Then the ducks started to quack, the bantams to squawk, and the peacocks to scream. All this time, as my voice went droning on about bells, blocks, jesses, leashes, creances and lures, Jezebel watched the proceedings from the interviewer's fist, quite unmoved. Now I was relieved that we only had one star! Fortunately when the film was shown there was a storm over the fells and we could see nothing on our television screens but a faint blur.

Our next TV appearance was more successful. Jake Kelly, who is one of my favourite interviewers, came over from the BBC in Newcastle to talk about the castle and the falcons. Jake is kind and tactful, and never interviews aimlessly, but sticks to the subject in hand. Jezebel posed beautifully and even sat on my fist while I rode Saladin. We had some lovely close-ups of her looking just as proud and fierce as her diminutive size would allow.

A few weeks after this programme, Jake arranged for me to be a guest compère on BBC TV's regional programme *Look North*. This was a little unnerving, but everyone at the studio was so kind, and with a producer like Malcolm Campbell I had little to fear.

Another time at our local ITV station in Carlisle, I had a brilliant idea—one of my many brilliant ideas which fail to work! My children always seem to make gods of anyone who appears on television and I knew that they would be sitting up late to watch, as Anthony and I can never get them to go to bed. At the end of a little chat that we had about children's pocket money, when I think I shocked everyone by saying that I didn't give them any, I only bribed them to be good, I looked straight into the camera and said "Amanda, Sapphia,

Ivan, Sebastian—go to bed!" I thought that coming out of the magic box, this would have some effect. It didn't! They just rolled about on the floor roaring with laughter, and then considerately stayed up to con- gratulate me on my performance when I got home. It only goes to show that the Big Mother technique using close-circuit television would be a hopeless failure!

When it became known that we kept falcons, one or two people brought us sick kestrels to look after. These birds were generally emaciated, their breast bones visible through their feathers, and their plumage dull. They were often too far gone to cure. All we could do was to feed them up a little and let them go. Yet we doubted if they would live for long. Unlike an animal, once a bird has lacked sustenance for too long, it is seldom possible to bring it back to peak condition. Sickness amongst our kestrels took the form of loss of balance, which the vet believed came from poisoning caused by seed-dressing. No doubt the birds had pounced on a mouse or vole which had already eaten the chemical, and absorbed the poison into their own system, in the process damaging their brains. The poisoning seemed to be cumulative. As they could not balance, of course they could not hunt. They generally only fluttered about the ground in an impotent way, and were so thin that they appeared to be no more than bundles of bones.

I shall never forget the first English kestrel which we tried to nurse back to health. She was bigger than our Indian birds and she must have been very young, for when she roused her feathers contentedly, which she often did, she looked like one of those fluffy balls which children make in nursery schools. Our own kestrel's eyes had a proud and fierce expression, but this new kestrel had great brown eyes full of tenderness and good nature. We called her Boadicea, and attempted to put jesses and swivel on her in the proved manner. But as her balance was so precarious, it meant watching her all the time both day and night, for the moment we turned our back we would find that she had fallen off her perch and was hanging rigidly upside-down from her jesses. When we had to go out Mrs. Wells, who had at first not been particularly fond of the falcons, began to take a motherly interest in Boadicea, and when she fell down, would eventually flick her up again with the greatest expertise. This obviously could not go on, as we were all becoming exhausted, although we did our watches in shifts. Boadicea was now waxing nice and plump, and her breast bone was no longer razor sharp, but obviously the brain damage was no better, and as she could not fly on to a perch she would still be a pitifully easy prey. For this reason we could not let her go. We attempted to put her out at hack in the mews, but the stone floor, in spite of the straw we had put down and the paraffin stove we kept burning day and night, was still too chilly. She began to shiver and we feared she was going to develop pneumonia.

It was then that Anthony hit upon the idea of Sebastian's playpen. Here Boadicea lived happily for weeks, although her mutes did not improve the look of the white-painted bars. Eventually we managed to train the dogs not to go near her. Naturally Clovis gave her a wide berth anyway, but as Crusoe was still not much more than a puppy it was more difficult to stop him taking rather a sinister interest in her. I was afraid that when she saw him sniffing round her pen she might die of apoplexy.

She was a sweet and cosy companion in the house

and would often sit on our shoulders while we did innumerable jobs. If we held her on our fists it was quite unnecessary to wear gauntlets. In spite of the fact that her talons were extremely long she never scratched at all, owing to the fact that for some weeks she had not been able to hunt or eat. Her beak too had become overgrown and was curling inwards in what appeared to be a painful manner. It would definitely have to be coped. We were afraid that when we operated on it, she might have a fit, but we had to take the risk. We hooded her, and Anthony held her gently but firmly against a cushion, pinioning her wings against her sides and drawing her feet back with her leash, while I snipped through the beak. We had providentially bought an extremely efficient pair of nail nippers, and I had success first time. I then shaped-up the beak with a little file. Boadicea seemed completely unmoved by the ordeal.

It was terrible to see a bird as proud as a kestrel unable to use her wings, and the obvious urge which she possessed to fly was a sad thing to witness. Time after time she would gain precarious purchase on the rail of the playpen, only to parachute back again, usually I am thankful to say on to the plastic mattress.

One day I was curled up on the sofa reading when Boadicea managed to leave the pen. After a pause to regain her confidence she began to fly from chair seat to chair seat. I was just thinking happily that soon we would be able to set her free, when with a supreme effort she flew on to the back of the sofa where I was sitting, and fell down into my lap. She was dead. After I had got over the first throb of agony I began to re-member a story of how an ancient parrot had been revived from death by a spoonful of brandy before being baked for 60 seconds in a slow oven. I went through the horrible drill of forcing brandy down the dead bird's throat but I could not face the ordeal of the oven. Instead I put her in the airing cupboard in a cardboard box. In the morning when I went to look at her she was as dead as ever. But this remedy is not as crazy as it sounds. Flicking through these pages it seems that many of our birds and animals have died violent deaths possibly owing to our ignorance and lack of experience in looking after them. But on the credit side I think that we have saved at least 50 birds, fledglings and baby chickens abandoned by their parents, and this was usually by using the heat treatment.

11 *Entertaining Royalty*

I will always remember the first bantam chicks that we found abandoned on the drive. Their mother had obviously been too young and irresponsible to hatch out chickens at all, for unlike the usual run of game bantams who make wonderful mothers, she had abandoned her little fluffy chicks only a few minutes after they had emerged from the eggs. When we found them it must have been about an hour later. They were small and weightless bits of fluff, already almost cold and quite stiff. I felt through the soft breast feathers, but the tiny hearts did not seem to be beating. I wanted once more to experiment with the heat treatment, so I laid the four chicks on a hot water bottle in a card-board box and covered them with cotton wool. Then I left them for an hour. To my amazement, when I opened the box I found all the chicks on their feet, cheeping loudly for food. Frantically I put some turkey-rearing pellets through the mincing machine and fetched a bowl of water. For the first few days the chicks would only feed when crumbs were placed on my finger, mixed with a little milk or water, but after a few days the little bantams, which are extremely quick to learn, were eating happily from their own saucers. Already there was a pecking order, and I noticed that one little red chick was always pushed aside. Later we transferred the brood to a chicken run which we had had specially constructed, and I am glad to say that they are still with us. The little red cockerel which was the last of all the chicks to come round, and which was always being pushed away from the food, is now so tame that he has become an abominable nuisance. He is always breaking into the larder, and smashing my favourite pieces of china, in his fury at being driven out.

We have had many more successes with abandoned chicks, but also a few failures. Once when a pigeon had been sitting on some bantam eggs, she let them drop on to the stone floor of the garage. I knew that the eggs were three weeks old and were about to hatch; so I put them under a hot water bottle. The chickens did hatch out, but they died soon afterwards. My other failure was with a sweet little bantam chick—an only child whose mother had been killed by a fox. This chick was extremely noisy and obstreperous, and the whole castle would reverberate with its chirps. It took it firmly into its head that the hot water bottle was its mother, and instead of lying on top insisted on crawling underneath it. One morning I opened its box to find it smothered. After this I used children's hot water bottles, which of course have to be filled up much more often. We have now ordered an infra-red lamp, but as lately we have become so much more adept at finding the eggs, I doubt if we will have much use for it.

Fledglings we found much more difficult to rear. Every spring the children brought in abandoned baby birds thrown from their nests because the parent birds believed that they were not strong enough to survive. Perhaps it was a mistake to try and rear these orphaned birds, but I have usually preferred the runt of any litter. Strangely enough, as far as dogs are concerned there is a belief among local shepherds, who are realists above all else, that the runt in a sheep dog litter always makes the most intelligent worker.

These fledglings always looked pathetically frail and defenceless, and however often the children brought them in to me I could not resist trying to help them. Like all babies they possessed a strong instinct for survival, and never stopped opening their beaks for food. They swallowed the ground-up chick crumbs avidly, but I made a mistake when I tried to give one small starling finely-chopped hard-boiled egg. Some of the white stuck in its throat and choked it. Soon afterwards it died. But in spite of a number of setbacks, we did rear the majority of fledglings. Perhaps this was against the law of nature and the theory of the survival of the fittest, but I could not have done anything else. I must admit now though, that I am beginning to dread the endless colony of fledglings which will arrive in the children's grubby hands next spring.

On the credit side too was a little owl which we had a few years ago in Spain. We found it run over on the road between Mijas and Malaga. Its wing was injured but otherwise it was unhurt. We took it home and kept it in a cupboard in our villa. It must have been very young, for it never stopped crying for food. We would spend most of every day, when we should have been lying in the sun and enjoying our holiday, hunting for grasshoppers, which the little bird devoured avidly. As my cook remarked with true Spanish realism: "So many hundreds of dead creatures to keep one alive."

When the owl was better we released it, but it hung around for many days, obviously hoping for grasshoppers. One day we came back to find our cook waving a dish cloth at it to make it go away. She obviously disapproved of so much "messing about with birds". The little owl did leave us that night, and never came back.

On the credit side too was the raven which a friend gave to us in Dacre during our third autumn.

The raven had been found on the wild tract of land known as Shap Fell, which is 1,600 feet in height. It had a damaged wing. Our friend tried to keep it in his garden but the bird's activities had evidently begun to annoy the gardener, and it was time for it to move on.

I have just found a newspaper clipping with the heading *Lucifer the Raven Becomes a Problem*. A problem was putting it mildly! Lucifer had become a nightmare! Because of his damaged wing he could not fly, but only hop about the courtyard, where he spent his time creating mischief. He showed his antipathy to the pigeons by collecting masses of twigs and rubbish and placing them in the plague stone that we kept for the pigeons' drinking water. Then he would perch on the side and let his droppings fall amongst the whole revolting combination. His next attack was launched against the bantams. We had a partridge-coloured hen and her chicks encased in a fairly heavy movable wire run to guard them from foxes and cats. With his enormous beak Lucifer tipped over the run and gobbled up two of the chickens. When Anthony found them, the little bantam was fighting furiously to protect her last chick. There was blood all over her plumage and the little chicken looked extremely groggy. I am glad to say that both the chicken and its mother recovered from this onslaught.

Lucifer was an accomplished thief. He would hide trinkets, as jackdaws do, and I once found my secateurs

The Great Hall—showing the South Window
Photo. Eric Davidson

Writing—with a little help from the family
Photo. Eric Davidson

Delilah, in proud mood
Photo. Border Press Agency Ltd.

amongst a pile of dogs' bones in an old chicken house which he used as his home. When he was discovered in some ghastly misdemeanour, he would retire to his den and make soft deep crooning sounds which were intended to be endearing. Although I often thought of asking the warden of the Tower of London if he would accept him as a gift, I never actually got around to it!

This diabolical bird also waged a permanent war against some climbing *Madame Butterfly* roses which I had planted to grow up our cherry trees. He seemed determined not only to eat the stems but to devour the roots as well. I covered the latter with rocks, but with his enormous black beak he rolled them back and continued his non-stop lunch. His next victims were the peafowl. Lucifer detested them. The peahens were terrified of him, but Nureyev made one or two attempts to stand up to him. The raven reciprocated by pulling the lovely eye feathers out of his tail. For a time after this we kept him shut up in his house, but his fiendishly ingratiating croaks depressed us to such an extent that we had to let him out.

We could see that Lucifer's damaged wing was improving. He could not only hop about but also flutter a short distance. His restlessness proved his longing for his own kind, and the call of the hills was obviously strong in him.

Although the raven was a fascinating pet to study, we had decided not to hinder him if he became well enough to fly away. We made it a rule not to keep any animal or bird against its will, and although we sometimes pinioned our birds on their arrival, once their feathers had grown out we never repeated the process. After he had been with us six months, we knew for sure that Lucifer was feeling the call of the wild.

One morning I was watching him dip his bristled beak into a bowl of raw beef and Winalot, of which he was extremely fond. In the middle of the meal he took six hops across the courtyard and made a few hoarse, brittle croaks . . . *kronk* . . . *kronk* . . . before he raised his pinion feathers. Almost before I realized it, he had taken off and was soaring above the battlements, away south in the direction of Shap.

We never saw him again, but I imagine that he is still soaring and twirling through the wind-tumbled heights, up amongst the lofty fells where he belongs.

In the spring it had been a fascinating occupation watching Juliet rear her chicks. She was now an excellent mother and exerted endless patience in teaching them to fly. I think that peafowl, like pheasants, do not particularly care for flying, and she had a difficult task. However, after about 4 weeks she was determined that all the chicks should learn to reach the top of the giant ash in the courtyard. First she would hop up from branch to branch herself until she reached the very highest one. There she would sit uttering piercing little screams of encouragement to her baffled chicks who were flurrying round the tree trunk. After a couple of hours of this she would return to the ground disgruntled, and sweep her children off to their nest in the nettle bed. After one or two nights the more dashing of the chicks had reached their mother on the topmost branch, but the less daring were still clucking in a flustered way at the bottom of the tree. Twice I saw Juliet fly down for them. After being prodded a few times the chicks would fly on to her back and cling there until she reached the top of the tree. At the end of a week there was still one little bird, a hen we thought, showing the white feather. By this time Juliet had become thoroughly bored with this particular offspring and had decided to abandon it. It was getting dark and the nights were cold. We were worried that the little peachick might die of exposure or fall prey to nocturnal enemies. Once more we decided that there was to be no survival of the fittest in the Kinsman zoo, and every night that week Anthony or Amanda, who both had good heads for heights, would climb up the tree and place the small ball of fluff under its mother's wing. Juliet was an extremely good mother on the whole, and even as the months wore on to winter we would see her roosting in the ash tree or the garage with her wings spread over her five 'teenage' children, who were now equally as big as she was. In the mornings she must have felt very cramped and stiff. That winter she got frostbite in one of her claws again. During the next few months we saw a gradual decline in her condition, and one day in January she quietly died.

In the spring, while we still had all nine peafowl, we were visited by Princess Sharada Shah, the younger daughter of King Mahendra of Nepal. The Princess was spending three weeks in Britain with her husband, Kumar Khadga Bikram Shah, as guests of the Foreign Office. The 25-year-old Princess had a degree in economics and English, and her husband, who was also 25, had just completed his law studies. I gathered that they wanted to visit the Lake District because our fells and woods and mountains are so similar to their own forest-clad slopes in Nepal.

After being received by the Queen on Tuesday, the couple were to travel north to Cumberland to visit the Outward Bound Mountain School on Ullswater. After that, the representative from the Foreign Office thought that it would be a nice idea if the Princess and her husband had a typical English Sunday tea with us.

From Harrods I ordered some Darjeeling tea, which apparently Princess Sharada Shah was fond of. I must say that it was extremely good. We had hot cross buns, and Sapphia and I made some of those chocolate corn-flake cakes in the shape of birds' nests and filled them with marzipan eggs and fluffy chickens. Luckily the Princess managed to keep one chicken as a souvenir, although Sebastian tucked most of them into his pockets as soon as they arrived on the table.

I was not sure how one should entertain a Nepalese princess in the heart of Lakeland. Eventually we borrowed an electric hare from some of our Romany friends and decided to have a whippet race between our two whippets and some of theirs. However, on the day when the Princess arrived for tea, the rain came down with monsoon-like intensity. On her visit to the Out-ward Bound School she had been lent a down-filled duffel jacket, but in spite of this her lovely sari was spotted with mud, so we cancelled the whippet race. Instead, the royal couple toasted themselves by the fire and chatted about the similarities between the Lake District and Nepal, both of which they thought com-pelling in their own way. I had been born in India and knew exactly what they meant.

We had thought very hard about what souvenirs to give our guests on parting. For the Prince we had a shepherd's crook, especially made for him by a local farmer, with hounds and a fox carved on the bone handle. For the Princess there was an old engraving of the castle as it looked in the 1800's.

As we shook hands with the Princess and her husband at the front door, we saw that the rain had stopped; the sun was glinting hopefully through the clouds. Taking advantage of the brief spell of sunshine, the peacocks were displaying themselves on the lawn. The Princess was amazed that we should keep these "vicious birds" in such close proximity to the house. In Nepal, she told us, peacocks are so wild that if they see human beings they fly straight for their eyes. I explained that in England peacocks had become so domesticated that they never attacked humans, and that they even put up with our small sons who, when they thought we weren't looking, made darts at their beautiful tail feathers and tried to extract them.

I don't think the Princess ever believed me, for at this moment those two vain creatures, Romeo and Nureyev, caught sight of the Princess's beautiful black Daimler glistening enticingly, with raindrops still on the bonnet. Their own looking-glass had long since been broken, and the lure of their reflections was irresistible. They screamed some encouragement to their hens, and then all nine of them alighted in a body on the car. Of course we immediately shooed them off, but to my horror, as the Daimler was being driven away, I saw deep scores on the lovely new shiny black paint.

The Princess took all this very well, and a few weeks later we received a very sweet letter from her and a present of a gold chaste cigarette box and match-box holder studded with coral and turquoise. These two little treasures have pride of place in the King's Room.

12 Winter at Dacre

THAT year, autumn's own small summer was spoiled by the Helm Wind, which tore at our poplars, our wild cherries, our sycamores and our oaks. Old brown leaves twisted and turned into the flooded beck, like the starlings and crows which twirled and rolled in the wind currents above.

In a few months, Jezebel's moulting season would soon be coming round again, and we wanted to let her go. Although she was flying well on her creance, and sometimes even flying free to the lure, she was for the majority of the time attached by her jesses to her perch. We hardly ever saw a bat any more, and now that Jezebel had been with us 18 months and had done her job, we did not particularly want to keep her in captivity. But we did not dare let her go. Most of the keepers around Dacre will trap, or shoot at, any hawks they see, for they believe them to be antipathetic to the rearing of pheasants. We had become too fond of Jezebel to take this risk.

One day in October, while Anthony was in London, our problem was solved for us in quite a horrible way. We had by now to keep our grain in the mews, as it attracted mice in the dungeons. Some sacks had just been delivered in the morning and I had signed for them without bothering to investigate. I had just finished cooking lunch for myself and the children, and was sipping my coffee, thinking as I looked through the window how lovely the vermillion leaves of the wild cherries looked as they whirled round and round the courtyard. It was then that I noticed that the door of the mews had been left open. I dashed out to close it, and to see that Jezebel was all right. In the space of two hours since the delivery of the grain, a cat must have got in, for hanging from Jezebel's leash and jesses was no more than a wing and a couple of claws. All I could think of at the time was of digging yet another hole under the weeping beech before the children found out. During the course of the evening I brooded for a long time. Naturally I blamed myself for not checking up that the door was closed, but it is difficult to be on watch all the time. It was depressing news to have to tell Anthony, whose bird she had been, when he came home that night.

That autumn we did some hectic shopping in Penrith. We were determined not to be caught by the snow as we had been the previous winter. We bought lots of electric light bulbs for the long winter evenings. Our big brass candelabra is pretty to look at, but rather unpractical, as the electric candle bulbs keep popping, and we did not want to be stuck with wax candles through the endless winter evenings. I stocked up with an extra batch of towels to soak up the rain under the windows. We also got in extra peat and firewood, and more oil for our central heating. We have six central-heating radiators in the Great Hall, and six in the King's Room. It costs us about £6 a week to keep that little lot ticking over. Our bedrooms are heated by electric fires. Originally we had hoped to install electric storage heaters throughout, but this would have overloaded the village. As it is, with my dream kitchen, built into walls eight feet in thickness, and sporting cooker, dish-washer and waste disposal unit, the strain on local power supplies is fairly substantial.

The previous winter we had left it too late to get first-class hay for the ponies. The hay delivered to us had been black and rather mouldy. But we were learn-ing. This autumn we had ordered our hay in good time. The bales, when they came, were a lovely golden colour, sweet-smelling and fresh. As well as the supplies that we had bought, we had an enormous stack of our own hay from the pond field. A few months previously we had laughed because we had heard a programme on the wireless about the only farmer left in England to harvest his hay in the old-fashioned way, with a scythe. For this was exactly what we did! When the haymaking season came round, we would be watching the sky with just as much trepidation as the farmers around us—probably more, as we had no drying machine.

That autumn we also laid in stores of pony nuts, oats, bran and demerara sugar for bran mashes to give to our horses after hunting, for we had just started going out with the Cumberland farmers and the Cumberland foxhounds.

A kind farmer also let us cut some lovely copper-coloured dead bracken for bedding. It is necessary to let this bracken die off completely before it is used, for in its dying condition it can be poisonous. Again in December, the yews and their back-drop of rough grass were shrouded in snow, and the snow masked the little track to the castle, so that we seemed to be living in a world of our own. Crusoe loved the snow, and he tried to get Clovis to play with him in it. But Clovis, possibly because of his hard upbringing, was too dignified. So

Crusoe played alone. When the flakes had stopped falling he would bound out and roll over and over in the glorious white fluffy covering. We had brought toboggans with us from London, and the children had a wonderful time flying down the steep slopes by which we were surrounded.

We had also inherited masses of pairs of hideous black Victorian skating boots, which fortunately fitted the children. When the water of the tarns froze over, we would take an enormous brush along to brush off the snow. Then we would skate, not by the hour, as we had in London, but from morning till night. It was all quite different to "Queens"; much more bumpy, but much more fun! I had once broken my arm skating in Battersea Park, so my pace was rather slow. But the rest of the family had some wonderful races.

Some of my roses were still blooming and we had a big silver bowl full of them on Christmas Day.

This was a happy Christmas! We had been able to plan it, and the children had exciting presents which were exactly what they wanted. I personally thought that their choice was horrific—it was hamsters! Far too much like mice for my liking.

We had bought four little cages, metal and not wood, as apparently hamsters chew their way out of wooden cages. Additional items included four exercise wheels and four nesting boxes lined with wood shavings. The hamsters were called—for no particular reason—Pinkpuff, Greensleeves, Nipper and Snowball. They were far too energetic, and during their exercise hours used to dart all over the room. Greensleeves used to be exercised on my writing table, but created terrible trouble by chewing up various pages of this book, which was written in long hand. As I consider these pages to be some of my most immortal prose, and as I can never remember what I have written even a few days previously, this was something of a setback! Snowball escaped into one of the large tapestries and lived happily between the webbing and the lining for some months. Amanda constructed a very good jumping course for Pinkpuff with her hurdles between a jumping lane of books. Pinkpuff loved it. Nipper found his way into the Bedford van and made a temporary home in one of the horse-hair seats. We put his open cage in the van with some tempting food inside. One morning we managed to recover him. He was going round and round on his little tread wheel.

Eventually all the hamsters made homes of their own, I think, beneath the floorboards, for on New Year's Day about a year later I swear I saw a little head peering at me, half-mouse, half-hamster. But of course Anthony, who had not seen the apparition, thought I had been celebrating too much on New Year's Eve.

Yes, we had a happy Christmas! But the pattern of the previous year was repeating itself.

February the 1st dawned bright blue, with a promise of spring. Anthony decided to spend a day on the fells exercising the dogs. I watched Crusoe as Anthony put on his lead, and thought how he had changed from the tiny puppy which had first arrived in its cardboard box. Then he had been no bigger than my hand. He was now fully grown, with fine pure lines. But better than this he had an affectionate and faithful nature.

I knew that Anthony had planned to walk twelve or fifteen miles—whippets need a lot of exercise, and become extremely restless if they do not get it—but by four o'clock when he had not come back, I began to grow uneasy. I went to the door of the castle to look out for the headlights of the van coming down Vicarage Hill, but there was no sign of it.

The wind had risen and I saw that a storm was raging over the fells and blowing down the valley. There was a new moon being tossed about by the leafless branches of the great trees round the vicarage upon the hill top, but it was soon obscured by the driven rain. The storm was now making a horrible noise among the rafters. We had once fixed an iron cowl above the useless smoking chimney of the hall, and had never bothered to remove it. It was now making a deafening sound as it twirled round and round. I sat on for another hour, becoming more desperate. The whole castle seemed to be shuddering with the blast of the wind. Yet above this pandemonium the clock seemed to be ticking derisively. I told myself that I was stupid to worry. There was nothing I could do. We only had one car. I had a motor-bike, but I was not anxious to take it out, even if I had had the slightest idea of where Anthony might be. It is possible to walk for 30 miles across the fells by Ullswater without seeing a living soul.

I drew the curtains. It was a relief to shut out the bleak landscape; those grim, black, jagged hills with the rushing clouds above them. I decided to do something constructive and put some milk on a low heat for the dogs. I also prepared hot rum for Anthony.

When at last Anthony arrived, he looked sick with worry. He was holding Clovis in his arms. He told me that the dog had collapsed on the fells. Crusoe followed at Anthony's heels. He was soaked, panting and shivering with cold, but otherwise seemed unhurt. Anthony said that up on the fells the blizzard had come swiftly out of the darkening afternoon while they were on White Stone Moor and miles from shelter. He had put on the dogs' coats and tried to hurry them home before the going became too bad; but soon the whippets, which hate rain, began to flounder in the mere that lay at the bottom of the scree they had to cross before regaining the van. Eventually Clovis collapsed, and as Crusoe was still keeping up well, Anthony decided to carry the older dog. The thick, sticky mud clung to his boots, and plodding through the bogs with Clovis' 30 pound weight made for slow going.

I gave the dogs their warm milk and put some brandy in it. Then we laid them on an eiderdown by the fire and rubbed them with towels to set their circulation going. Oddly enough, after an hour Clovis seemed more composed. He left the fire, curled up on the sofa, and went to sleep. It was now Crusoe who seemed to be in a state of collapse. The eiderdown where he had been lying was soaked through, and the water still seemed to be literally pouring out of him. I began to think that it must have been only sheer determination which had helped him home!

All in a space of five minutes the little dog did not seem only to be wet and shivering, but his eyes were becoming glazed. Although it was late, I decided to disturb the vet. at his home and ask for help. While I was talking on the telephone, Crusoe started to show the symptoms of a fit, and I explained these to the vet. He told me to put a cold cloth on Crusoe's head to calm him, and to bring him to the surgery in the morning for an injection.

Anthony and I built up the fire and took it in turns to sit up through the night. I will never forget the feel of that clammy cold cloth and the fragile little bony head beneath it; or the sticky feeling of the stiff body that was still expelling water on the eiderdown. Although

Crusoe went on having fits throughout the night, he never once tried to bite us. At last it was 8.30 and time to go to the surgery. The children would be late for school that day. The vet told me, I suppose to comfort me, that my little whippet would survive. When we returned home I put him on my bed and went to sleep beside him. On waking up, I found that he was dead.

That afternoon, Clovis, who seemed to have made a fairly good recovery after his ordeal, began to have trouble with his skin. It came out in peculiar lumps and abrasions. We took him to the vet who diagnosed poison. Where had he picked it up? We had no idea. Naturally, we now linked the poisoning to Crusoe's death. The cold and rain alone would have been unlikely to account for the collapse of one dog and the death of another. I heard by chance some weeks later, from a farmer, that up on the fells where dead sheep are sometimes not buried, the carcases are occasionally poisoned to kill foxes and other predators. It was possible that our dogs had eaten such a deadly feast. But this was only supposition. There was one other possibility. Most of the labradors, and some sheep dogs around Dacre, are fed on dried meat. It had been highly recommended to us. Twice in the previous week, when we had failed to get fresh ox cheek or heart, we had fed our whippets on this meat, which was reported to be so nutritious. Perhaps it had been too nutritious! A whippet's blood heats up much more quickly than that of a labrador. Possibly the meat had been too rich for them. But this, again, was only supposition.

It was an unlucky coincidence that the poison should have begun to work on the dogs' systems at the same time as the storm blew up. Otherwise we might have suspected poison in time to have had their stomachs pumped out.

That evening, after we had buried Crusoe, I sat for hours gazing into the grey dusk across the fells. They looked like great prison bars of iron. They echoed back all my depression and desolation.

After about a week, Clovis recovered completely and was quite himself again. Yet, although he was only a young dog, his muzzle turned quite white during the seven days of his illness.

Perhaps this has not been a particularly suitable story for this book, which I had intended to be light and escapist in character. But it might help someone else to avoid falling into the same trap as I had done. Although I had been brought up in the country, in Ireland, I think that after my years in London I had developed a towns-woman's idea of animals. I think I had even credited my dog with a soul! Animals are too vulnerable to become attached to in this way. In the "real country", where shepherds often put a stone round the necks of their sheep dogs to drown them when their working days are over, it would be considered ridiculously senti-mental. Animals in the country are liquid assets.

But I could not help missing my little whippet terribly. For a whole year he had been my constant companion. He had sat for hours with me in the snow while I took photographs of the castle under its new, glistening coat. He had guarded the place when An-thony was away. He had slept at the foot of my bed and made a doormat of himself in the kitchen while I cooked the meals. Now I could hardly bear to look at the child's high-backed Queen Anne chair where he usually lay with both eyebrows raised in perpetual surprise . . .

Like something inevitable, bad luck pursued us. The next events were, in their way, almost as depressing as the death of Crusoe. I would have preferred to have interspersed them with amusing anecdotes, but this is the sequence in which the events occurred, and I think that in a book of this type, deviations from the truth are boring, and exaggerations and lies are instantly detectable.

A few months after we had lost Jezebel, one or two of our bats were beginning to creep back, and we decided to send for two more falcons from abroad. A red-headed merlin and a lagger, which is almost identical in appearance to a saker, were our choice.

Once more we spent hours in careful preparation. We had to make sure that the mews was clean and dry and free from draughts. Since the death of Jezebel, the mews had undergone yet another transformation and had been turned into a loose box, So we had quite a job, mucking it out and re-painting the walls.

The red-headed merlin was to be imported from India. When she arrived we saw that she bore a faint resemblance to our English merlins, but was more heavily armed, having a thicker beak and stronger claws. She was a dainty, gentle little thing, and did not seem to need any *manning*, but sat quietly on our hands, or on her perch, from the start. When she was fully trained we saw how beautifully she stooped to the lure. Although so small, she was the noisiest falcon we ever had. She hated the peafowl, and when I carried her around the garden on my fist she would scream at them in absolute fury. She was fed on sparrows, mice and a little beef.

As the lagger was a much larger bird—this one weighed 2 pounds 1 ounce—Anthony decided to bring it down from London himself. The train was crowded, and as the falcon was incessantly bumping around in its box Anthony gave the guard a large tip to put the container in a safe place in his van. When he came to collect it in Penrith, he found the box covered with a heap of mail bags.

Half an hour later we had the dented cardboard box in the mews. In a warm corner behind a screen made from a candlewick counterpane was a rather elaborate perch, of which I was inordinately proud. The screen was cut from a red suede coat of mine. This coat had certainly seen better days, but trimmed with a defunct embroidered bell-pull, it looked rich enough for a sultan's palace. The suede was practical too, as there were no threads to drag at the falcon's claws.

Carefully, Anthony raised the corner of the lid. In spite of the mail bags the bird was undamaged. She looked huge in comparison to our kestrels and our merlin.

Anthony pinioned her wings and carefully lifted her from the box. We were working by the light of a single candle, but before I covered her head with a silk handkerchief, I had a fleeting but definite impression of our new lagger.

Her breast feathers, white-gold as desert sand, were streaked with umber. Her eyes were huge, black-brown and blazing with fear. She had murderous claws which tried to clutch convulsively at my hands as I nervously fixed her jesses—a job that unfortunately could not be accomplished in gloves. Then, after fastening the swivel and leash, still trying to avoid the slashing talons, our new acquisition was tied to her perch. Once settled, she took one look at her jesses and began to shriek *eek-kra-ik*, *eek-kra-ik*. Between screams, with sudden furious movements, she attempted to tear them off. We decided to

Moby Dick, our white homing budgerigar
Photo. Robert Armstrong

"The menagerie is growing." Left to right, foal Nimrod, Sheba, two pigeons, Clovis the black whippet, Columbine the donkey, Delilah our Saber falcon, two racing whippets Foxy and Misty, and Saladin, Anthony's fell pony
Photo. Sunday Express

Our modern kitchen within the 8 ft. walls

Photo. Eric Davidson

leave her for a while in darkness and went back into the castle to put ointment on our cuts.

This time we spent three days and three nights on the watching and waiting routine. During the first 24 hours our difficult bird never stopped baiting from our fists. After 48 hours she was settling down but was still refusing to eat. Owing to her temperamental disposition Anthony called her Delilah. By the third day, much to our relief, she had accepted her first piece of raw beef-steak, and by that evening she was entirely at home on the falconer's glove, *rousing* frequently and standing on one leg, tucking the other contentedly into her feathers. This is always a good sign.

By the end of one week Delilah was a reformed character. She had avidly consumed a mouse, a pair of pigeons, and a saddle of hare.

After her meals she would always look wonderfully contented and would *feak* busily for half an hour. Delilah was always alert and keen for her food, and her castings and mutes looked healthy. Her eyes too were round, wide open and bright. There were only two things which worried me about both our new falcons: their legs and claws were not losing the unhealthy white colour which they had had on arrival. As we realized from their nightly session on the scales, they were also failing to gain weight.

At the end of two weeks we could scarcely believe that Delilah was the same bird that had glared at us with such fear and hatred on her arrival. She was now crossing the length of the mews with one flap of her wings, to land on Anthony's baited fist with endearing confidence.

Anthony intended to take the lagger's training seriously. A friend of his, who did not subscribe to the misconception that a falcon would drive away his game, was interested to see Delilah in action on his grouse moor. After another week she was flying on a creance, a hundred yards of fishing line. After a few more days she had graduated to a lure that I had made for her. This was a messy-looking thing constructed from a heavy horseshoe, with leather stitched over it, then covered with pigeons' wings and scraps of meat. But it was effective. Throughout her training Delilah was also taking long walks on the glove. After five weeks the job of *manning* was practically finished.

But it appeared that I was as accident-prone as ever! Anthony was working late on some business letters, so I undertook the job of feeding the bird—a job which in any case I loved—and then took her down the newel stairs to her mews, a candle in one hand and the heavy bird perched on the other with the leash wound in the appropriate way round my fingers. Perhaps there were still one or two bats left on the stairs, although I had not seen any for weeks. But Delilah seemed to be excited. When I opened the large oak door and carried her into the windy courtyard something horrible happened. She gave a sudden jerk, wrenching the leash out of my hand. Then she was free!

I caught one glimpse of her long, powerful wings silhouetted against the full moon as she soared down-wind over the slates of the mews. Then there was nothing more. It was useless to whistle, or to swing her lure in the darkness. She had a full crop and was content to be free.

All night I lay awake thinking of our lovely lagger hanging upside-down from some tree caught by her jesses, struggling frantically in rage and terror, her primaries broken and useless—struggling there in the howling wind on any of those thousands of trees on Dunmallet or Vicarage Hill, until she died.

At dawn the wind had dropped and I went into the garden and began a rather aimless search, already knowing, with a sense of foreboding, that I would not find her.

Delilah was sitting on the topmost branch of the highest tree in the moat! She was on one leg, her plumage close and sleek. Her crop looked full, her eyes were alert, and her moustache was bristling. She, unlike me, had evidently had a delightful night!

When Delilah saw me she looked at me amiably enough, but she had tasted a night of freedom and now evidently had no intention of coming down.

I spent a disheartening three hours holding up a piece of enticing beef for her. She ignored it. I was just going to dress the children for school, Anthony having kindly cooked the breakfast, when the thing that I had dreaded happened! As soon as she saw me leaving, Delilah decided to join me. Perhaps she had smelt the bacon frying. But as she flew down, her leash caught on the high, fragile branch on which she had been sitting, and twisted round it. My heart stopped beating while I watched the headlong dive, the wild flurry of pinions, and then the limp swinging body. The bird hung head downwards 40 feet above me. But Delilah was a bird of character, and after regaining her breath she managed to clamber back into a sitting position.

Now for once I had an extraordinary stroke of luck. During the previous hour I had noticed a stranger working on the building of the neighbouring Dacre Castle Farm. Just at the awkward moment when Delilah was hanging by her jesses, he came up to watch proceedings. I greeted him in rather a surly way, dreading the inevitable question: "Is it valuable?" But the man only said to me quietly:

"I can't untie her. The branch is too weak for my weight. But if ye'll fetch a saw, I'll cut it down."

Now this tree, a lime I think it is, is the highest tree on our policies. Could the man be a steeplejack? I went to fetch a saw and to tell Anthony the news. As it happened, he was not a steeplejack but Cumberland's champion pole vaulter and a great all-round athlete. He certainly performed a feat of which Tarzan might have been proud! Anthony managed to catch the branch as it came down, so breaking Delilah's fall, and within a few seconds she was sitting on his fist, contentedly rousing her feathers as if nothing had happened.

For the next few weeks the lagger's training continued and on the first of February Anthony flew her at a rook on a stretch of open country nearby. She made a kill in fine style. The little merlin took a starling a few days later.

We were winning!

13 *Going to the Dogs*

THIS, our third winter in Cumberland, was to be the worst that we had yet experienced. By the middle of February it had become so cold that everyone at Dacre Castle had gone into a state of semi-hibernation. All outdoor activities ceased. Pale-grey clouds drifted silently over the fells. The nights came down prematurely, loud with the rue of the Helm Wind.

We heaped logs and peat in the huge fireplaces, piled more eiderdowns and blankets on the children's beds, and bought more paraffin in Penrith, for the stove in the mews. We felt we were ready for the worst that the northern winter could bring. Yet the steely stillness of the sky produced an ominous sense of further tribulation.

The blizzard started with large gritty nodules of snow and ice that rattled against the latticed panes with such venom that I thought the glass would break. In fact one pane in the children's room did splinter, and although this was two years ago I have not yet been able to find anyone who is expert enough at fenestration to replace it. I have been told that the whole window must be removed and the lead melted. This is not a cheerful thought! The snow settled nowhere, but scattered and fled before the wind.

We went to the fells to take hay and nuts to our horses. Up on White Stone Moor the snow felt as hard as pebbles as it lashed against our faces, yet even here it did not settle. It raced in the wind, through the empty skulls and the bleached bones of the sheep that had died by the water courses during the previous autumn.

Every day the cold seemed to increase. Our fingers became numb and rigid as we cracked the ice in the horses' drinking trough, before running back to the van to warm ourselves with a thermos of hot tea. The horses themselves seemed fairly unmoved by the blizzard. They had grown coats like fluffy teddy bears, together with lovely long whiskers.

About this time we noticed that the lagger and the merlin were looking rather seedy. In the past when we had gone to the mews to feed them they had been in the habit of *mantling* and *warbling*, but now they scarcely seemed to see us. Their heads drooped, their eyes were vague and sunken, and sometimes they were sealed. They seemed to have little appetite, and their mutes were discoloured. In our own minds we diagnosed aspergillosis, a kind of pneumonia, which can sometimes be caused by dusty or damp conditions. The mews was clean and extremely dry, but the falcons seemed to be slightly short of breath, and we thought this might be due to the fumes from the paraffin stove which we had been forced to keep burning day and night owing to the unnatural cold.

That evening we moved the birds into the castle and dosed them with an old-fashioned remedy, rhubarb boiled down to the consistency of yellow syrup. During the next few days the falcons continued to sit hunched above their swivels, with their wings drooping. We obtained the advice of two veterinary surgeons, but neither of them offered us any other remedy than those we had found in our manuals.

The vets and the manuals advised an infinitesimal dose of bismuth carbonate, but by this time the birds had sore throats and froth around their beaks. To dose them was a messy and discouraging task.

Even healthy hawks harbour a few resident parasites, mainly red mites, but when the birds become ill these increase. While I was dosing the little merlin I noticed that something horrible was happening. Red mites were crawling from the bird on to my hand. They had evidently felt the bird's body cooling. A few moments later the merlin died.

Poor Delilah lingered on for three more weeks, her feathers becoming more ruffled, her expression apathetic, her eyes usually sealed. She still stepped confidently on to our hands for her nasty doses of bismuth carbonate, or black peppercorns, or whatever we were trying to give her at the time. But one day we knew that she would step on to our hands no more. She had gone to her own trouble-free refuge.

Disease and ignorance had combined to defeat us when we tried to care for our lagger and our merlin. I know now that the weeks of struggle to save the lives of these two birds were doomed from the start. A great number of these imported birds are affected by aspergillosis in the wild, and as their lungs are slowly destroyed, they become less efficient in catching their prey, and so fall into the falconer's trap, in search of food. The disease then becomes precipitated by removal to a cold climate.

Never again will we attempt to keep an imported falcon. A few weeks after Delilah's death we were given a kestrel with a damaged wing. She has been with us two years. She is not a particularly nice or good-natured bird, but since her arrival I have never seen a bat in the castle and I now believe that they have become completely extinct here. Our English kestrel often pecks at our hands and scratches them with her talons. She has definitely proved *haggard*. I think that next summer, now that her primaries have grown again, we will definitely hack her back to the wild.

In the spring, the talk in our favourite local *The Salutation* was all of whippet racing. Penrith, unlike most northern towns, had no whippet racing club, but the situation was soon to be remedied, and Anthony and I were on the newly-formed committee.

"Aye, but ye'll be hard put to find a track," grizzled a miner from Workington, an old hand. "The council 'll never approve it."

A tall man stood up to get his mug refilled—strong, all drawn from the wood. He was our old friend Ned of High Burnthwaite. He was a good-looking fellow with enough Romany blood in him to spill over into his features.

"I'll get you yer track," he said quietly. "Ther's a nice little field across the junction, near the scrap and metal yard."

Anthony and I knew the place well, up by the Penrith town head. This was the stamping ground of many of our Romany friends. When we walked through the narrow streets up there I swear that we often smelt the intoxicating aroma of roast hedgehog, although of course none of our tinker and potter friends, even in their most unguarded moments, ever admitted to eating this morsel.

"Who is going to do the handicapping?" I asked.

"Mr. Groggins to be sure," said an Irishman who was working on the new motorway. "Has he not been the handicapper for Kirkby Stephen for many a long year?"

The Irishman had been in England for only eleven months, but in that time he had attended every whippet race meeting between Workington and Pontefract. He certainly knew his onions. There seems to be some affinity between Irishmen and long dogs.

"Aye, yer right," said an old shepherd from Ullswater, dressed in an ancient but extremely elegant moleskin waistcoat. He lifted his glass expertly, his grey beard spilling into his ale. "I'd say Groggins was the best handicapper south o' the border. I'll propose him as chairman and secretary of the new Penrith Whippet Racing Club."

Mr. Groggins, a tanned, rugged-featured man with a grey bristling moustache, grinned benignly and patted his beautiful whippet Cato Street. He was scratch dog along the whole of the west coast. He wagged his tail feebly and went on dreaming in front of the flames of the peat fire. Anthony seconded the motion. The resolution was passed.

The Irishman drank noisily from his tankard of beer.

"What'll the system be? Your 28 pound dog'll be off one yard no doubt, and your 27 pound dog off two. That's if your course is 200 yards, to be sure."

A small ginger-haired man with a nut-cracker face, was crouching on a settle in the corner of the old chimney recess. He held a small tawny whippet on his knee.

"Aye, and bitches 'll be pulled a yard. That's the rule." His small ferrety blue eyes were twinkling, and glancing at his whippet again I saw that it was a dog and not a bitch. He caught my eye.

"That dog o' yours 'll be too big, no doot."

Recently Anthony had been given a beautiful blue whippet called Misty. Because of his propensity to wander, he had been in danger of being put down.

I bridled: "Not at all. He only weighs 27 pounds."
This was not strictly true. With a day on lean meat we
could just squeeze him in at 28 pounds, but this of
course was part of the strategic game.

"An' that black un o' yer husband's. It'll be a mite big
too. It's the little dogs is all th' fashion now, yer know."

"Well," I rallied, "perhaps we'll get a longer track."
Tracks were always 250 yards in the olden days.

Now the whole of the whippet-racing fraternity
began to break in with advice. Everyone in *The Salutation*, it appeared, knew everything there was to be
known about whippets, and soon the old smoke-
blackened beams and the rough whitewashed walls rang
with the shouting of men and the barking of dogs. Yes,
there was a lot of merriment and good cheer in our
local that evening. It was fortunate that the landlord,
an ex-guardsman, was fond of dogs, for everyone at
the meeting had brought his "treasure" with him.
Taking up the argument, the tawny whippet began to
snarl at Clovis, who pricked his one good ear, raised his
hackles, and bared his fangs.

"And what'll ye' be feedin' 'em on?" baited my
sandy-haired friend. "They'll win on nothing but beef-
steak and raw egg yer ken? And they'll need a drop
of brandy too, or they'll be left at the post."

"Old wives' tales," I said firmly.

But I was already having terrible visions of our home
being run on the lines of a home in a typical mining
town—porridge for the children and fillet steak for the
dogs. And this, as it turned out, was not far from the
truth. Though with fairly good results! For in spite of
my friend's depressing prophecies, Clovis won his first
heat at the opening meeting a month later, and thanks
to Anthony's careful training he and Misty now have

four cups between them, as well as a number of second and third rosettes. I feel that they were worth all the trouble that we spent on them.

When I was asked in a television interview at the opening meeting what was the point of all this, I explained that it was just like owning a miniature race horse, but even nicer because one trained the dog oneself at only a fraction of the expense, and even if whippet racing now is only a shadow of the powerful sport it used to be, there is still a great deal of excitement to be secured from it. The dogs themselves adore it. They bark frantically before a meeting, until that wonderful moment when they are put into the traps.

On Jack De Manio's programme I tried to describe what it was that I liked so much about whippets.

In the first place they have a singular beauty of form and outline, combining grace, muscular power and strength. They are alert and extremely intelligent. They can gallop over 250 yards at a fantastic speed, and this is a wonderful thing to watch. I personally subscribe to the school of thought which believes the whippet to be a miniature greyhound and not a greyhound crossed with a terrier. Many famous works of art, from Van Dyck's charming canvasses right back to the paintings of Assyria, bear out this theory.

But above all, whippets are gentle and sweet dogs about the house, charming to children, true and loving companions. I also quoted the neat set of points laid down by Dame Juliana Berners in the Boke of St. Alban's: *The head of a snake, the neck of a drake, the foot of a cat, the tail of a rat, the side of a bream, and the back like a beam.*

The press soon took up the saga of the new whippet racing craze.

Whippet racing loses its cloth cap image, announced one paper. And *Bunty joins the whippet racing set*, screamed another.

We got a lot of fun out of these articles but even more fun out of the racing itself. There was something incredibly exciting in watching the racing performance of the whippets, which are, after all, a small version of the oldest hunting dogs in the world.

There is the thrilling moment when the whippets spring from their traps, and you wonder if your own dog, in spite of his heavy handicap, has a good start. The few tense moments—alas, over all too soon—as the four dogs in their various coloured collars gallop at terrific speed up the course to the rag or the lure. The amazing burst that the little dogs put on as they jack-knife, sometimes almost as much as 15 feet, on to the hare (which is nothing but a piece of sacking). The marvellous moment as you see the coloured flag go up for your own particular dog. Or the sinking feeling in the pit of your stomach if it doesn't, which probably means that your dog has been seen to *wurry*, or attack the dog in the lane next to him. In such a case there is a re-run without the offender, and you leave the field in disgust, to start your dog's solitary training all over again.

While on the subject of whippets and greyhounds, I can see, when I look up from my writing, a portrait in oils of Coomassie painted in 1877 by the well-known animal painter Harry Hall. This painting belonged to my uncle. It once hung in New Abbey in Ireland. It was given to me by my Aunt Winifred when my Uncle died. It is now hanging in the Great Hall of the castle in the most honoured place that we can give it.

Coomassie, who once belonged to my Uncle's father, was definitely the smallest and probably the most famous little bitch ever to win the Waterloo Cup. She only weighed 42 pounds and won the cup quite brilliantly on two occasions. I remember this picture of the lovely little fawn greyhound and her kennel companion Winchelsea, from the days when I was only a child and a guest in my Aunt's home, one of the most lovely Georgian houses in Kildare. Perhaps my love of long dogs stems from those early days.

The Penrith and District Whippet Racing Club is now well-established, with more than a hundred dogs competing in the handicaps. But unfortunately no permanent site has yet been found. The field "up the junction" is much too steep and rough for a permanent track, and permission to stage the races on the football field has been turned down by the Urban Council on the recommendation of the Parks and Open Spaces Committee. The members of the club are evidently considered undesirable!

Brilliant yellows. Opaline sky-blues. Emerald greens. White-winged cobalts. A vast flock of jewel-coloured budgerigars, flying against a dark velvety background of trees. I first saw this startling sight five years ago, a few miles from Dacre in a wild garden belonging to our landlord Major Hasell, and his charming wife. A friend of ours, John Strutt, an expert on liberty budgerigars, had for a time been an agent to the Hasells at Dalemain, their lovely part-Georgian, part-Elizabethan house. During this time he had kept his birds in an aviary in the pretty, wild garden by the beck, amongst the daffodils, the narcissi, the forget-me-nots and the hundreds of different varieties of conifers.

Two years ago at Dacre Castle, a visitor would also have been welcomed by these beautiful, brilliantly-coloured little birds, flying free and nesting in the trees around. For John had given us eight birds from his homing strain. To these we had added a dozen untrained birds bought at a pet shop. John advised us to choose fairly streamlined birds, and not the short-tailed chubby type, as the former are much better homers. We also had to plump for the more natural colours of plumage, the colours of the wild birds as found in their Australian habitat. Emeralds and turquoise blues were our favourite choice; not the more delicate homebred varieties—the mauves, the whites or the greys. Birds with red eyes, fallows and albinos were also to be avoided.

When we were living in Paris on the *Annie Laurie*, we bought some tiny exotic birds with plumage of emerald green and sapphire blue. Disaster struck when they had their first bird bath. All the colour ran out of their feathers and they turned into perfectly ordinary little finches. We managed to get them through the customs successfully and put them into a lovely, roomy antique gilt cage in our house in Pelham Crescent. These little birds gave us endless enjoyment, but always nagging at the back of my conscience was the thought that this way of life was not right for them. I disliked the concept of caged birds and I felt that these little birds should have the opportunity to fly free, to nest, and to rear their young. It was a heavenly moment when we opened the door of the cage and saw them soaring into the sky, before swooping down into the high branches of a lime tree at the end of our garden. We subsidised their feeding for a few days and then saw them no more.

Ever since that time I have never kept a bird in a cage. But our budgerigars were liberty budgerigars, free to come and go as they pleased. They flew around the garden and surrounding countryside all day, and only returned to their aviary in the evening, called down by their cosier and more domesticated friends the stay-at-home birds, who refused to leave the aviary.

We had chosen the site of the aviary with a great deal of care. It was under a spreading apple tree, screened from the winds and blown rain by rhododendrons grown in tubs of peat. The flight was to face south. The aviary was of a fairly simple design built by a local carpenter. The wood had been creosoted and allowed to dry; we did not paint it, as paint of any kind is deadly to birds. Both the aviary and the flight were raised on stout wooden legs to minimize the danger from rats, and the flight was covered with a fine wire mesh outside the wooden framework, to keep the mice at bay. A little sliding trap-door was then fitted into the side of the flight as an exit, and a small funnel placed in the wired roof as an entrance. Just beneath the funnel was a wide perch on which we would balance a plate of seed, as an extra lure to attract the birds home in the evening. The dimensions for our aviary were roughly as follows: Flight, 7 feet long by 5 feet wide by 6 feet tall. Shelter, 4 feet long by 5 feet wide by 6 feet tall in front, and 4 feet tall at the back.

Budgerigars naturally nest in a hole in a tree trunk, but as we had only one or two of these ancient trees in our grounds we hoped that our birds would accept the next best thing—a nesting box, entered by a hole in the front. They did! By the end of the first breeding season which started in the third week in March, our little flock had almost doubled its numbers. Some families consisted of as many as six chicks, but we preferred the smaller broods. Six chicks seemed just too many for the little hens to manage, and they became overtired and seedy. Once more our local carpenter did a magnificent job. He constructed 16 small boxes to our specifications, about 6 inches square and 7 inches tall, made of thick hard-wood with a concave bottom board to hold the eggs. These boxes were hung round the outside flight, and it was imperative to set them on the level to avoid a series of rather nasty fights among the hens, who all wanted to be top bird.

I was rather horrified when I first saw the baby budgerigars. They were so unlike our lovely fluffy bantam chicks and ducklings. Untidy bits of fluff stuck to their pink wrinkled skin. They looked rather like baby reptiles, mottled and gaping. They also developed extremely slowly and stayed in their nesting boxes for at least 30 days. Yet after a week the change was fantastic. They were transformed from little toad-like creatures to gem-like mites, darting about the aviary.

I think that our success in rearing our budgies may have been partly due to the extremely careful diet sheet which we prepared for them. Canary seed, white millet, pannicum millet. Green stuff for the adolescents that have not yet flown free, and little boxes of cress were also extremely popular. In addition, the birds should have cuttlefish bone, grit, and a mineral block. And of course a water fountain. Bunches of millet sprays and finely-chopped hard-boiled eggs are a great treat too.

Although some of our birds were trained homers when they arrived, we followed our usual policy and kept the whole flock shut up in the aviary for two weeks before opening the trap. But what an exciting moment that was! The homers popped out of the exit like well-trained soldiers, before soaring away on jewelled wings. I had a horrible sinking feeling as I saw some of the more daring ones fly straght towards

Vicarage Hill and Dunmallet. But by 5 p.m. they were all home again for their evening meal, fluttering round and round the branches of the old apple tree and queueing up at the entrance funnel. During the next breeding season, many of the more daring hens abandoned their nesting boxes and found roosting places in rotten trees by the beck, and in the village gardens where they picked up interesting tit-bits. But they usually called on us sometime during the day for a meal. These birds were intended to be the first budgerigars to actually breed in the wild in Britain.

There is a huge ancient oak in the parkland in front of the castle, with a very fine hole in its trunk. This was the home of one particularly pretty hen and her two chicks. It was a delightful sight to see the three little birds pencilling vivid lines of blue and green across the sunset as they soared, already strong on the wing, straight back from the aviary to their nest.

"Lady, have yer lost a budgy?"

Countless times I have been asked this question by thoughtful strangers knocking at the front door. They have seen one or other of our birds soaring round the battlements. It always took me a long time to explain that these particular budgerigars were free to come and go as they pleased.

Another question that we were often asked was how do the budgies get on with other wild birds? The answer is—perfectly! We have seen them sharing bits of bread and cooked fat with our peacocks, our ducks and our bantams, wild starlings, crows, sparrows and blue-tits, with never a quarrel.

And what of predators?

Cats are our biggest problem, and whenever we see a cat leaping from the apple tree on to the roof of the aviary, we shoo it off. Falcons have never worried us much. I doubt if kestrels would attack a budgie anyway. They are more interested in mice.

But fireworks now! They are another matter, as we learnt by bitter experience!

Last November there was a Guy Fawkes party on the village green. In the morning there was not a single bird in the aviary and I have never seen one of that particular flock in these parts since. Fortunately all the birds had been accustomed to the wild for at least two years and I had no fears for their survival, but how I missed their gem-like colours flashing in and out of the apple boughs as they came into the aviary at night to rest and eat and roost!

Now we have stocked up with eight new homers, as I could not bear to see the aviary empty. But we are going to be extremely careful to shut the exit trap when the fifth of November comes round. These hardy little birds seem to be able to survive snow, wind and tempest without batting an eyelid. But fireworks—no!

14 *"We Louve this Castle Well"*

DRIFTS of snowdrops were appearing in the moat. Against their dark green leaves they looked whiter than the snow itself. Soon every small chalice in the castle was full of them. This spring, our fourth in Dacre, the wild cherries we had planted were coming into their own, and frothing with white blossom. On the wild bare regions of the fells where the wild thyme grows on slopes to the sky, the curlews were calling, a sure sign that spring was truly with us.

Spring, that first week in March, meant only one thing to me—spring cleaning! Fortunately the paint-work that year, thanks to our damp-proofing methods, was perfect. But there were various other problems like polishing chandeliers, mending tapestries and rugs, and scrubbing-down yards and yards of stonework. Then we had to turn out the dungeons, sweep down about a quarter of a mile of newel stairs, clean out the pigeon loft, shine up thousands of panes of leaded glass, and brush teak oil on enormous lengths of oak beams. Mrs. Wells and I had to clean the four turrets, each as big as a separate house, and then the central keep— five houses in one. The castle is full of statues. All these had to be scrubbed. I found an old tooth-brush handy for this job. And even after the inside of the castle was finished, there would be the out-houses to whitewash, the fences to creosote, the lead gutters to clean.

I preferred work in the garden, for while I toiled I could see the plants coming to life. I love watching things grow.

My herbs were some of the first little plants to send up new shoots in the spring, and this was a special treat for me after years of cooking with dried herbs in London. Very soon I knew we would be having fresh mint sauce with our lamb, and the new tiny leaves of thyme and sage with our chicken.

When we first saw Dacre Castle there was a handsome stone salting trough near the front door, which I had felt at the time would make a splendid herb garden. Between the time of our signing the lease for the castle and our moving in, it had disappeared—stolen I suppose. But during the last five years we have managed to pick up some very fine salting troughs from farmhouse sales. They look beautiful in the courtyard and outside the back door, and in them I have now arranged my herb gardens.

I felt instinctively that herbs were somehow right for the castle. Had not Charlemagne had 75 herbs growing in his grounds? So why not the Lords of Dacre?

I do not have green fingers, but my herb garden seems to be flourishing in almost embarrassing profusion. My father—who *had* green fingers—gave me some roots of fuzzy apple mint with which to start. They are spreading like wild-fire. I then bought a dozen more herbs in Penrith market. They seemed to me such friendly, adaptable little plants. They are all doing well, and our salads cups, pot roasts, omelettes and forcemeats have improved beyond recognition.

The hardy perennial, lovage, is a herb that I cannot

do without. The young tender leaves taste exactly like celery, and are excellent in stews or *bouquet garni*. The blanched stems too are delicious, cut up in apple and walnut salad.

I also grew fennel, but abandoned it as it tasted too much like liquorice.

Then there is salad burnet, another perennial. It has a cucumber flavour and is very good in long cool summer drinks.

I planted sorrel too, which dates back 3000 years and gives a tang to salads, or particularly oleaginous stews.

Rosemary is a lovely little evergreen herb with leaves like pine needles. It is marvellous with roast lamb, but I have found it rather delicate unless taken indoors.

Chives are a *must*, and look very smart chopped up and mixed with cream cheese.

Lemon thyme and thyme always remind me of hot summer days. I would not be without them. I generally make thyme jelly for the winter. It is delicious with hare.

I found rue a dead loss; perhaps our soil did not suit it, but it was terribly bitter.

Chervil, with its lace-like leaves, makes a pretty decoration for almost anything.

Then naturally I have plenty of sage.

And lastly a mysterious plant called Good King Henry, because I loved the name. But I never found out what it tasted like because it got tangled up with the weeds!

The garden was at last taking on some semblance of order, and the task of making it from the stony shambles that we had found five years before was almost complete.

Almost the prettiest part of our grounds now was the wild garden round the pond. Here Anthony and I had

planted masses of daffodil and narcissus bulbs of every
description. They looked charming under the blossoming apple trees in the early spring. After that came the
pretty red flowers on the bushes of *cydonia japonica*,
which positively seemed to thrive in clay. Then the
briar roses came into their own, especially Nevadas and
Ladies of Penzance, which flourish in rough grass. After
that the lilacs and *clematis montana*, which we grow up
all our tree trunks. And lastly the *buddleias*, ablaze with
red admirals in late August.

The mountain ash which we planted four years ago
has at last reached the children's bedroom window. In
the autumn the gentle tapping of its orange berries
against the leaded panes of their window lulls them
happily to sleep. In olden times these trees were always
planted by every Cumberland house. They are supposed
to give protection against the forces of evil. Even the
yew trees which I thought, when I planted them, would
only be likely to give pleasure to a future generation, are
now head-high. Our cypress hedge will actually need
clipping next year.

We have planted climbing roses, wistaria and clematis
around the old grey walls of the castle which have
withstood a hundred sieges, and they are flourishing,
climbing up and caressing the great rugged stones with
a curious tenderness.

But there are still a lot of things in the garden that we
have not yet got round to. My orchard at the moment
consists of only six fruit trees. I want many more. I
would like a vegetable garden and about a hundred
more varieties of roses. But I am glad that there is still
so much to accomplish, for I have an uneasy feeling
that the planning of a garden is probably much more fun
than the completion of it.

I only hope that I am here next year and not living in a city again. There are so many country pleasures and endless things to do.

There is "pot hunting" for the children, for in the summer we take Leprechaun, Pixie and a little Shetland that has been lent to us, to pony shows and gymkhanas. At the moment the pink walls of the children's bedroom are covered with nothing but thirds and "specials", but there is always room for hope. Then there are auction sales in old country houses, where one can sometimes pick up a pretty bit of old pottery or china for a few shillings. Sometimes there are fascinating bits of Staffordshire, fragments of tapestry, or ancient embroidery amongst piles of junk. Recently we picked up a splendid snuff box made from a ram's horn decorated with a pewter fighting dog, the type of thing that used to stand upon the bars of old pubs. At a sale on the North-East Coast we found a pair of scrimshaws. These are walrus tusks with black-stained carvings scratched into them by the sailors of the old whaling boats. These things have for me a distinct tang of the sea, and the rugged way in which the whales are drawn on them, together with the lines of longitude and latitude, enhance my fancy.

I am now collecting a somewhat unusual type of dinner service; it is made up of odd plates of old china, bought for a shilling or two. This gives me a lot of amusement at sales and antique shops. I have never been able to keep a formal or matching dinner service without breaking some of the pieces and spoiling the set, and now I will have no more worries in that direction.

I am too squeamish to care for blood sports, but for Anthony and indeed most of the men round here there is the most reasonable shooting and fishing in England.

I love hunting, but more for the brilliant hues, the crisp frosty mornings, and the sight of the huntsmen and hounds and fine horses, than for the hunting itself. I am one of those deplorable people who hunt to ride, rather than ride to hunt!

Then there are drives to the Lakes, even more lovely in the winter, than in summer. They are at their best in isolation. One day, when the children are old enough, we intend to have a sailing boat on Ullswater, which for me will be a sort of floating studio.

I am writing these final pages on a cold night in December, and we have been preparing for another Christmas. Outside is a white world, but in the King's Room, where I have my writing table, everything is cosy, thanks to the roaring log fire.

It is nearly midnight, and as I write I take occasional drinks of a hot toddy that Anthony has made for me. In the very depths of winter we often have one of these drinks to warm us up late at night. *Grogs, nogs, punches, bishops, toddys*—the very names seem to crackle with cosiness and goodwill! Somehow they seem so exactly right for Cumberland. My toddy tonight has been made in a pewter goblet, one of six, a present from my mother. This too seems exactly right, so vividly does it recall the thought of Christmas and of conventional Christmas cards of huntsmen and squires in pink coats and flowered waistcoats, drinking their punches in front of log fires, surrounded by crimson curtains and candelabra.

The room seems homely and deeply peaceful, and the high sandstone walls give to it all the benison of age. There is nothing more lovely than natural stone walls, provided that the stone is of an attractive colour. Perhaps people buying old cottages should remember this.

Ultimately it is more economical to strip the walls to the bare stone, rather than plaster or paper them.

And think how much one saves in decoration!

How glad I am to get away from those wallpapers of my childhood; monotonous phantasmagorias, spread across the walls of hotel bedrooms or nurseries! How well I remember those awful raised patterns, pinched and prissy, of straggly pink flowers on buff or cream. Or those fiddly michaelmas daisies spread across the walls of countless South Coast boarding houses like leprosy. Or those awful nights spent counting pagodas and khaki-faced geisha girls until a bleak sun dawned in a chilly sky.

My sister said something delightful about the King's Room when she visited us:

"Why, it looks as if you had lived here for years!"

I knew exactly what she meant. Had we had enough money when we moved into the castle, we would no doubt have decorated it with the reverence we felt for the long history of what is probably the oldest castle in Cumberland. We would have attempted fidelity to the period in which the castle was built. We would have furnished it with nothing but solid oak, heavy wrought-iron, with a few concessions to the Jacobean period, possibly a stump picture here and there and heavy four-poster beds. All these things would have been excessively uncomfortable, and the four-poster beds, much as I love them, impossible to make. And then how ridiculous and anomalous my modern kitchen and streamlined bathrooms would have looked against this museum-like mediaeval background. In any case, how far should one go? Rushes on the floor and nothing but joint stools to sit on?

No, I am glad we could not afford all this, for I find

that the King's Room makes a perfect setting for all our treasures. Treasures, known and loved—a storehouse of finds from many ages and many countries. In this room that has known the passing centuries, nothing that is beautiful in itself seems to look out of place. Ours is a collection of antiques evidencing the accumulative rather than the consciously discriminating. But I love it all the more for that.

For instance we have the darkness of English oak in a fine glowing refectory table, and a carved court cupboard with scenes from the life of Christ. One finger of an angel is so beautifully carved that I can sometimes spend whole minutes in contemplation of it. When the removal men carried this cupboard up the stairs they got it stuck halfway, and only some huge glasses of whisky gave them the impetus to get it to the top. They have informed us that if ever we are thinking of leaving the castle, they will without doubt be on another job!

Then in the King's Room is the burnished gold of Venice and Florence, a carved casone and a lantern-like chandelier with angels round the base, casting a benediction on the room. Our only French pieces are two Louis XV chairs with original tapestry covers. Fortunately for our bank balance I am not fond of French furniture. The scrolls and squirls of its ormolu remind me too much of the scrolls of icing sugar on a sickly-sweet birthday cake. Flemish craftsmanship is represented by our tapestries of golds and blues and greens, repeated in the seventeenth century cabinet inlaid with warlike scenes in ivory and tortoiseshell. Even our Georgian crystal lustre candle-holders on each side of the ancient fireplace do not seem out of place. In fact they look positively ethereal against the pale stone walls.

One of our chief worries had been to find a suitable bed-back for the chapel room. As we could not afford a fourposter we took the plunge and bought a sixteenth century Flemish oak over-mantel for £12. Of course this could have looked incongruous as a bed-back, but like all truly authentic antiques it immediately fitted in. Indeed I think it looks extremely fine with its dark glowing eagles and lions and bunches of grapes.

As I write in the King's Room, I am amazed at how much that is oriental has fitted in too. The central theme of the room is set by a cobalt blue Chinese carpet. Translucent Chinese amber dragons, dogs, and griffins glow against the window, and a Korean wall scroll carries on the theme of deep blue and amber.

Other tiny things look perfect too—a fragment of carving from a Buddhist temple, a stone Madonna which stands on a disused corbel bought for £2 from a church that we saw being pulled down in Bruges, and a crumbling sandstone griffin bought for 10s. at a junk sale.

By the south window stands my one extravagance since we first moved to Dacre Castle. It is an eighteenth century blackamoor; the kind of blackamoor that the great ladies of Venice had modelled in wood and gesso after their pages. His gold and blue coat glows in the candle-light, and he is obligingly holding out a plate of fruit. I bought him a few months ago in London and I was determined to bring him north myself unless any harm should befall him. The marble base was to come up separately by pantechnicon. An Irish porter waltzed him up Euston platform and stood him upright on the floor of my sleeper. Unfortunately when the train started to move, he wobbled. In the end the blackamoor slept on the bunk and I sat up all night!

It looks as if you had been here for ages.

If the King's Room looked like that when my sister first visited us, now it looks even more so. For it is "lived in". Small acquisitions have crept in since that time, now almost taken for granted and melting unobtrusively into the general decor. The early Staffordshire bullbaiting group left to us by an uncle in his will, because he always knew we liked it. Another inheritance, an oval portrait of a good-looking great uncle of Anthony's, a Black Rod. I had wanted an oval portrait for ages—they always seem to look so well in film sets! Then there is the little Dresden monkey band. It is growing, because Anthony's mother has been collecting these little musical monkeys for us piece by piece over the years. The lovely sixteenth century carved wooden Madonna picked up at a country sale; we rather think it is Spanish, and mean to find out some day. The finger is off one hand and I have it somewhere in a drawer. I really must stick it on. There is a set of the Kaiser's wineglasses, looted by Anthony from the winter palace under fire from Russian guns. They were in store for ages but are now brought out and put on display. Then there is the sweet miniature above the fireplace. It is of a young girl dressed in grey and green, the daughter of Napoleon's surgeon. She was left to me by my dear father. Admiral Surgeon Skelton, Napoleon's doctor on St. Helena, was an ancestor of ours. Napoleon once wrote that he was the only Englishman he ever liked. Other Napoleonic relics have crept in too: a pair of red and gold glass decanters presented to Napoleon by his son-in-law Joachim Murat, the King of Naples, and a sad little statue with Napoleon's body and an eagle's head; he sits on a pile of history books with a broken sword at his feet. Then there are the little sixteenth century tiles and the pieces of Sunderland lustre which we started to collect at one time. But it is impossible to list them all. We only know that we are cosy and at peace in this room. And while there are still roses in the garden, the silver bowl on the sofa table will be kept full of them.

One or two snowflakes are now drifting across the great latticed windows as I write, as softly as the breast feathers of swans.

I feel strangely contented in this old sandstone keep, that for so many years has kept its solemn watch over the little village of Dacre. At one time I know the romantic unreal atmosphere of the building had taken possession of my thoughts, but now I realize that it means us no harm. Now I can even laugh at the superstitions I felt three years ago. I know that the castle is our friend, and I hope that it will remain our world for many years to come, and that those fells that surround us, bleached now under the moon and the myriad of little wet stars, will guard us for ever more.

There is only one thought that hurts me now. It is that everything cannot stay just as it is. Life is so perfect at the moment, with a few pigeons in the turrets; the peacocks and the bantams roosting on their beam; the ducks huddled on their pond; the budgerigars dozing in their aviary; the children tucked up in their beds under enormous goosefeather quilts. And the dogs dreaming by the fire. Sadly they must all grow up and become old.

Yet when I see the apples and pears on the blackamoor's plate—fruit grown in our own orchard—and when I hear the crackle of logs cut from our own trees and smell the scent of the late-flowering Iceberg roses from the bowl on my table, grown from our own rosebeds, I feel an ultimate faith in the bounty of God.

As the Earl of Sussex said so many hundreds of years ago:

"*We louve this castle well.*"